Higher Self Expression

How to Become an Artist of Possibility

HIGHER
SELF EXPRESSION

How to Become an Artist of Possibility

JEFF CARREIRA

ISBN: 978-1-7352650-0-1

Emergence Education Press
P.O. Box 63767
Philadelphia, PA 19147
www.EmergenceEducation.com

Cover and interior design by Silvia Rodrigues

"I am large, I contain multitudes."

—Walt Whitman,
Leaves of Grass

"Many poets are not poets for the same reason that many religious men are not saints: they never succeed in being themselves. They never get around to being the particular poet or the particular monk they are intended to be by God. They never become the man or the artist who is called for by all the circumstances of their individual lives."

—Thomas Merton,
New Seeds of Contemplation

Contents

Foreword

The Most Cosmic Superhero of All!

I WORK IN A SCHOOL OF HUMANITIES at a research university. I live in the heart of the academy with good, smart people. I admire them. I could even say that I love them. Honestly, in their fierce focus on class, race, gender, and sexuality, I consider them to be our modern-day prophets. Which does not mean that they are saints or perfect in any way. But they speak truths that much of the public does not, cannot, and will not hear.

But there is something of profound centrality and importance missing here. My university world, like much of the public culture, assumes a mostly materialist worldview. I suppose it works well enough. Actually, it works pretty darn well, as long as one concentrates completely on, well, what is working. We can build all kinds of cool gadgets and create new technologies, even life-saving vaccines (I'll stand in line). The problem is that all of this working-well comes at a tremendous, really devastating cost: the cost of us.

The whole shebang of Western academic, technological, and scientific culture, after all, operates with precisely the dualistic assumptions that Jeff Carreira urges us to look and experience beyond in these remarkable pages. Jeff does so from the depths of his own spiritual search and long meditative experience of the "ultimate Oneness that is." He certainly has a way with words, like all effective spiritual teachers: "Chopsticks, however adeptly employed, cannot be used to eat broth." Dualism cannot grok unity. Unity is not a "thing" to know out there somewhere. One cannot in fact "know" it at all. One can only become it, be it. And there is the crux, the crux of every great mystical or meditative tradition when we try to translate or force-fit such a Oneness back into our ordinary ways of speaking and thinking (including scientific ones).

We can't.

But we try anyway. Jeff uses language to get us outside of language. In the process, he has come to realize what so many previous thinkers and writers (from Gertrude Stein and William James to Philip K. Dick and Thomas Merton) have realized: that the very best thinking and writing is not done by a conscious agent, but rather flows through a minded body and a social space in a particular kind of ecstatic experience; that we are always in fact authoring ourselves, even as we are also being authored; and that we are all, together now, "one co-emergent, evolving life form." Those are all wow-claims, but Jeff offers them up in these pages with grace, humility, and a well-read learning.

There is so much more that I could say about this little book. Three things seem particularly important to say up front and immediately in a Foreword like this.

The first is Jeff's admirable refusal to surrender his realization of consciousness as such or the awakening of those exotic energies in the human body, that brilliant white light that the Hindu Tantric traditions have theorized and symbolized as "kundalini." This double commitment to a Conscious Energy or an Energetic Consciousness does not always sit well with this or that religious teacher. Indeed, many a contemplative tradition would encourage us to ignore the energies and their paranormal effects and concentrate instead on the consciousness alone. But Jeff does not do this. Jeff surrenders, twice. Jeff pays attention, twice. And that makes all the difference.

The second thing that strikes me as especially important to emphasize here is Jeff's call for what, mythically speaking now, he calls a new School for Modern Mutants. Jeff is a teacher. He organizes and leads what is a self-described Mystery School on-line. This is the real subtext, or supertext, here. But the mythical framework is more than appropriate, and probably the only remotely adequate means to express what is really going on in these pages.

Everything, all at once.

I get a lot of email from people who have read this or that book of mine and have found some reason to write me about their extraordinary, and often traumatic, lives. They have suffered. They have been awakened. They no longer fit in. But they want to. But not into the old ways or conventional culture. They have mutated. They are looking for new community and practical guidance, particularly around the activation, stabilization, and development of anomalous abilities. There are very few places or people I can safely recommend to such super-readers. Jeff Carreira is one of them. He has been there. He knows (or is). And now he teaches and guides.

The third aspect of this book I just love is very much related to this second one. I am referring to Jeff's warm embrace of American popular culture. Popular culture is where we explore who we really are and how our cultures might yet express us, all of us. It is where we place our fears and doubts, our convictions and intuitions, and, most of all, our real-world paranormal powers in "safe" fictional forms. It is where we get away, just a bit, for imagining who we really are, for realizing, if usually only unconsciously, "that something much more profound and vast is living through [us] right now, and always has been," as Jeff puts it in his opening pages.

This particular pop-paranormal aspect of the book is crystallized in Jeff's final realization that his first spiritual teacher was not Thomas Merton but Captain Marvel, "The Most Cosmic Superhero of All!" as the November 1973 cover announced his advent to us searching kids. I remember the exact comic he writes about. I bought it, too. I was eleven. I lacked Jeff's cosmic experiences of consciousness and embodiment, his realization, as both a kid and then as an adult, that the entire universe is his real body. Alas, the comic was all this Jeff had.

But now I have this book. We all do. We also have Jeff Carreira. We have a humble cosmic mystic of nondual consciousness and evolutionary energies. We have the real deal.

Jeffrey J. Kripal
31 December 2020
Richmond, Texas

Introduction

IN THIS BOOK, I WILL bring light to a miraculous discovery. This book is about the realization that you're not living your life as the person you think you are, the one who has your name, who was born on your birthday, and who shares your memories. It is about discovering that something much more profound and vast is living through you right now, and always has been. It is also about the possibility of giving up control of your life in a way that will allow your true and highest potential to live through you.

This may all sound a bit abstract, but the journey you are about to take with me will introduce you to some remarkable men and women who have pursued—and even realized—this same possibility at different times, in different ways, and in different places. In this book, you will learn about some of these artists, writers, philosophers, scientists, and spiritual luminaries who devoted their lives to higher self-expression. It's my sincere hope that you will see aspects of yourself, and your journey, in them and theirs.

Years ago, during the early dawn of my own search for life's meaning, at a time when the light of deeper truth was barely beginning to break through the haze of my traditional life, I came across a small book that explained the four fundamental questions. I don't remember much about that book now, forty years later, except for one thing: I remember vividly that the first question was "Are You the One Who Is Living You Now?" (John 11).

I didn't have a profound awakening upon reading this question, I just found it a bit curious. I remember that the book went on to explain how our lives are always being lived by a divine source and that it all made sense to me. What I couldn't have guessed was how central that question would become to how the rest of my life unfolded.

As my spiritual life developed, I became obsessed with the possibility of surrendering my life to a higher source. I had come to understand that my traditional sense of self, the person I knew myself to be—with my name, my birthday, and my memories—was only a small part of who I really was. I began to have experiences that opened me up to my higher Self, and each one fueled my fervor for more. The trajectory of my life became largely guided and shaped by my passion to fully express and embody my higher Self.

As the years passed, I pursued a path of discovery that often didn't make sense at the time, but when traced back reveals an arc of realization that began with my academic background in science. From there, my path took a sharp turn into a life of spiritual dedication in which Eastern enlightenment traditions were interwoven with my love for Western philosophy. Now, I want to share the fruits of that journey with you, and use my story and interests to illuminate the unique and powerful path of higher Self-expression that has been explored by pioneering souls for thousands of years.

The first draft of this book was written in three weeks. I had been doing some research and was planning to write a book about becoming an Artist of Possibility. I imagined that it would take six to eight months to write, but once I sat down, I couldn't stop. My process of writing, and the mysterious energy that drove me, is one of the things that I write about because it exemplifies certain aspects of what the art of possibility means to me.

An Artist of Possibility is someone who expands the realm of what is possible. You will also, hopefully, discover that you are one, which is why you were interested in reading this book in the first place. Artists of Possibility create through a profound spiritual process of manifestation that I call creative illumination, but which is also called between-ness, active imagination, and the imaginal, by others.

This book was created through a process of creative illumination. The book itself wanted to be written. It coaxed me into writing it. The energy of the book entered me and drove me to write a draft in three weeks, and writing this book was a transformative event for me. I've realized more and more that writing this book has changed me. It has opened me up to a new range of possibilities in my life. That is what happens in the mutually transformative process of creative illumination. The artist creates art while the art creates the artist.

You were born to create a possibility that wants to come into this world through your life. The possibility of what you are here to bring into the world was the energy behind your birth. It brought you into being so that you could express that gift to the world. You probably already know this, or at least suspect it. You know that you possess the possibility to deliver *something*, and you want to offer it to the world.

In reading this book, I will ask you to practice what Samuel Taylor Coleridge called the "suspension of disbelief." You will be asked to let go of the idea of an objective world described by facts. You will be asked to let go of the ideas of time and space, and even of your own independent existence.

Instead, I want you to relate to your life as if the whole thing—past, present, and future—is happening right now. The possibility that you were born to bring about is squeezing into existence right now through your whole life. It feels like it happens little by little over time, but I want you to imagine that it is all happening simultaneously.

That is also how I suggest you read this book. Yes, you will have to read it one word after another, one chapter, and then the next. And along the way, you will gain information and understanding. But if you walk away from this book with only some fascinating information and new understandings, you will not have received the full value it contains.

This book is more like a mosaic than a journey; it contains pieces that together comprise a story. But when you have finished it, you will discover that the real meaning is *beyond* the story. While you read the book, allow yourself to be coaxed into your own co-creative process. Allow your imagination to actively see yourself in everything that is written here. Don't just read it. Relate to it. Allow the book to read you, while you read it. Let yourself engage in a mutually transformative process and, in the end, you will see that a new possibility for your life has been shining through each page simultaneously at the same time that you will see how it shines through each moment of your life simultaneously. My gratification in writing this book will come from knowing that the possibility you were born to bring to life has arrived for the world.

CHAPTER 1

Habits and Higher Mind

OUR JOURNEY BEGINS WITH GERTRUDE Stein during her years as an undergraduate student at Radcliffe College, the sister university to Harvard College in Cambridge, Massachusetts. The precocious young Stein would go on to become a towering figure as one of the central characters of an amazing circle of writers and artists in Paris during the first decades of the twentieth century. In this role, she would support and cultivate some of the most prominent figures of the emerging modernist movement, including Pablo Picasso, Henri Matisse, Ernest Hemingway, James Joyce, F. Scott Fitzgerald, and many more. The more I've learned about Gertrude Stein, the more impressed I've become with her influence and vision.

But our story starts long before Stein moved to Paris, at the time when she was doing experiments in the psychology laboratory at Harvard while working under Hugo Münsterberg. Münsterberg was an experimental psychologist from Germany who had been invited by the great American psychologist William James to oversee the psychology laboratory. He and James both considered Gertrude Stein to be a model student.

Stein was involved in research with a fellow student and colleague named Leon Solomons. Together, in 1896, they published a paper called "Normal Motor Automatism" in *The Psychological Review,* on their results. Although Stein only played a secondary role in the writing of this paper, she would publish a second paper independently two years later called "Cultivated Motor Automatism," in which she reports on her continued research in the same area. Later in life, she would back away from the results of this research and some of the claims she made at the time, but would nevertheless maintain that it revealed the beginnings of what

9

would become her signature style of experimental writing.

The research Solomons and Stein had been doing centered around the automation of certain human processes and activities, most notably, writing. They knew that many human activities could be completed unconsciously—for instance, it's possible for us to get dressed each day without paying any conscious attention to what we're doing—and they wanted to determine what the limits of normal automatism were. Up until that point, motor automatism had only been studied in hysterical patients. They wanted to explore how many different human activities could be accomplished unconsciously, and how long those activities could remain unconscious to the one performing them. Could, for instance, the activity of writing be performed unconsciously—beyond the deliberate control of the will and intentions of the writer? And, if it could, for how long?

Their experiments involved a board mounted on rollers or hung by ropes from the ceiling so that it could move freely. The subject of the experiment would rest his or her hand on the board so they could write while avoiding strenuous muscular effort. In some experiments, an act of writing would be initiated, such as the repeated writing of a letter of the alphabet, and then the subject would be asked to direct their attention to the reading of a novel. Stein wanted to see if the writing, once initiated, would continue even when the person's conscious attention was withdrawn from the hand and focused on another activity.

One of the things they found over and over again in experiments such as this, was that once the test subject became aware of any automatic movement of their hand, it was nearly impossible for them not to willfully take back control of it in some way or another. Imagine that a test subject's hand was set in motion writing the letter 'A' over and over again. While their attention was lost in reading the novel, they were not aware of what their hand was doing, and so it was free to move of its own accord. But if for some reason, they became aware that their hand was moving, it would stop. Once a subject became aware, they would instinctively override the movement. In "Normal Motor Automatism" Solomons and Stein state emphatically that: "This tendency to stop automatic movements and bring them under the control of the will is very strong. Nothing is more difficult than to allow a movement of which we are conscious to go on of itself. The desire to take charge of it is almost irresistible" (496).

This assertion, in particular, struck me because it relates very much to the way I learned—and now teach—meditation, and gives me a powerful way to understand why people have so much difficulty following the instructions for meditation. Those instructions ask people simply 'not to make a problem' out of anything that arises in their mind during the meditation. They are instructed to simply sit still, relax, and be OK with anything that happens without reacting to any of it, in any way. The difficulty people have with this form of meditation is that, just like in Stein's experiments with automatic writing, they find it nearly impossible not to take charge of whatever is happening.

The theory of meditation is simple enough. You just sit still, relax, and pay attention to everything that unfolds without getting involved with any of it. When you try this, what you find is that absolutely nothing changes. Everything that you were experiencing before you were meditating keeps on going. This includes the arising of thoughts, feelings, and memories, but it also includes all of the more deliberate activities of thinking, judging, and drawing conclusions. It all just keeps going on, just as it had before. Even the sense of being yourself and involved with it all doesn't change.

In meditation, most people find it fairly easy to be comfortable simply being aware of the arising and falling away of random thoughts. Even the occurrence of feelings and emotions is generally not too difficult to learn to relax into. But once a person sees the more deliberate activities of thinking, judging, and concluding going on, they find it all but impossible not to take control. We assume, at an unconscious level, that these activities cannot go on without us because *we* are the ones doing the thinking, judging, and concluding. Once we see these things happening in our minds, we inevitably find ourselves getting involved with the process either by trying to stop it because we believe it is antithetical to meditating or by trying to guide the process in a direction that we believe will be more beneficial. Either way, we have moved out of the position of being a passive observer to the phenomenon of our mind, to once again being the willful agent of it all. We have stopped meditating.

In Gertrude Stein's experiments with writing, I see the same essential challenge of meditation but with the complicated twist of adding movement to the practice. Imagine that you are a test subject in one of Gertrude Stein's experiments. You are seated at a table and your right arm is resting on a board that sits on rollers. There is a pen in your hand touching a piece of paper. The trial starts, and Gertrude Stein invites you to relax. She gently moves your arm so that the pen traces the letter 'G.' She keeps repeating this motion over and over again for a few minutes and then stops. Now she moves to your other side and directs your attention to a book that is perched on a stand, open for you to read. It is a novel of your choosing and Gertrude asks you once again to relax and begin to read.

As you read the first few lines on the page, you feel Gertrude moving your arm in the same motion she had before. But soon, you become engrossed in the reading and are no longer aware of your arm moving. The book is a spy novel and the person who was just introduced seems suspicious. The description of the Bucharest hotel in chapter two where the spy meets the army captain is captivating and you picture the beautiful woman in the blue dress as your former girlfriend, Josephine.

Suddenly, for some reason, you notice your hand moving. You look over and you catch a glimpse of your hand tracing out the letter 'G.' As soon as you notice that your hand is moving of its own accord, it stops moving. For a short instant, you had the disturbing feeling that you had lost control of your hand and that it was writing all by itself. It felt separate from you in an odd and disturbing way. Gertrude instructs you to turn your attention back to the book and forget about your hand. You go back to reading and soon forget your hand again. Eventually, you notice that it is moving. You reflexively look at it and see that it has written out a few words that came from what you were reading. And, once again, after a momentary and disembodied sense of your hand acting of its own accord, the hand stops.

How relaxed would you have to become before you could notice that your hand was moving and watch without stopping it? Could you relax enough to just observe your hand as it wrote all by itself? You would be engrossed in the novel, then notice that your hand was moving and witness it writing without stopping it or taking control of the activity. You would have no volitional or intentional connection to what was being written, in fact, you wouldn't know what was about to be written until you saw it on the paper. You would be reading at the same time that you were writing. It would feel as if your hand had come alive and was writing all by itself.

This was the kind of automatic writing that Gertrude Stein was studying; how well could people be trained to allow the body to act beyond their conscious control? Stein was not only a researcher but also a subject, at least in the first study, and it seems that she got very good at automatic writing. In fact, she got so good that her report says she stopped needing to use a novel to distract herself and, instead, simply read what she wrote, following three or four words behind her pencil.

What Gertrude Stein was fascinated with was what she called our "bottom nature." She believed that, if we could remove our conscious involvement, each of us would find that there are a set of activities that our mind and body could do perfectly well without us. These included conditioned and habituated activities that would continue to enact themselves without the need for the intervention of human will.

These automatic actions are like the idling of a car. If you remove your foot from the gas pedal, the car engine keeps running at its idle speed. Stein imagined that human beings also have a kind of idle, a bottom nature, that would continue to run once we removed our conscious control. She believed that uncovering the bottom nature of individuals would reveal that there were certain fundamental types of human beings that were programmed into the nervous system below the level of consciousness.

But what initiated Gertrude Stein's interest in experimenting with automatic writing and the underlying nature of our being, and how does that interest relate to her later artistic and literary life?

Stein gives some indication in her book *The Autobiography of Alice B. Toklas*, which is, in reality, an autobiography of herself, but from the point of view of her lifelong companion, Alice. In the book, Stein mentions her experiments with automatic writing and her essays published in the *Psychological Review* saying that, "It is very interesting to read because the method of writing afterwards to be developed in *Three Lives* and *Making of Americans* [two of her early novels] already shows itself" (78).

To gain more insight into what might have been motivating Stein's interest in automatic writing in the first place, we need to look at the influence that her mentor, William James, might have had on her. While Gertrude Stein's research was directly supervised by Hugo Münsterberg, James had a much greater influence on her at the time. "William James delighted her," Alice/Stein says in the autobiography (78). James, she claimed, always taught his students to keep an open mind.

So fond was Stein of James, that she once asked herself, "Is life worth living?" And answered herself, "Yes, a thousand times yes, when the world still holds such spirits as Professor James" (qtd. in *Meyer 212*). Clearly, William James had a tremendous influence on Stein, and it is impossible not to assume that his influence extended to her work in automatic writing. After all, by the time Stein was doing her studies, James had already been passionately interested in similar research for decades. By exploring our bottom nature those aspects of ourselves that go on mindlessly without conscious attention or deliberation, Stein was exploring what William James often spoke about as our "habits."

William James published his psychological masterwork, *The Principles of Psychology,* in two massive volumes in 1890. Two years later, he published an abbreviated summary of his ideas in a book called *Psychology, A Briefer Course.* Both of these titles included extensive discussions of the role of habit formation in the human psyche. And Stein would undoubtedly have been very familiar with these ideas at the time she began her research in 1896. But for our purposes, it is easier to look at James's writing on habits from a book published in 1899 called *Talks to Teachers on Psychology.* This later work presents James's core ideas on psychology in simpler terms and in ways that Stein was likely learning from him at the time.

In a chapter called "The Laws of Habit," James states emphatically that, "Ninety-nine hundredths or, possibly, nine hundred and ninety-nine thousandths of our activity is purely automatic and habitual, from our rising in the morning to our lying down each night" (*Writings 1878-1899* 751).

We are, according to James, "mere bundles of habit, we are stereotyped creatures, imitators and copiers of our past selves" (751). He goes on to say that, "all our life...is but a mass of habits–practical, emotional and intellectual..." (751).

In his earlier work, *Psychology, A Briefer Course*, James explains that the habits that make up almost all of who we are, reside in our bodies. An act performed many times over eventually becomes a habit. Once a habitual behavior has been established in the body, each muscular movement triggers the next muscular movement in a chain that completes the action. These habits enact themselves without us even knowing it.

At first glance, this might strike us as a bit depressing. After all, the fact that the vast majority of what we do every day is almost entirely the result of the unfolding of unconscious, habitual patterns doesn't immediately seem like a compliment or a reason for celebration. But James did rejoice in this fact, because in it he saw the key to human growth, freedom, and happiness. The fact that most of our lives occur completely unconsciously is a blessing as long as we "make our nervous system our ally instead of our enemy" (751). We need to use the laws of habit to our advantage by making as many beneficial activities as we can automatic and habitual as early as possible.

The greatest cause for celebration is that our bodies and nervous systems appear to have been constructed to be habit-forming machines. We live our lives on a foundation of unconscious habits (our bottom nature, perhaps?) and we can work consciously to establish the best possible habits for our life. As James puts it, "The more of the details of our daily life we can hand over to the effortless custody of automation, the more our higher powers of mind will be set free for their own proper work" (751). This is a key part of the developing theory of higher Self-expression.

In order to look deeply into the full implications of the laws of habit that James outlined, we will need to spend some time with another of his protégés, John Dewey. Dewey never studied formally with James, but he did take a course with James's close friend and collaborator, Charles Sanders Peirce at John Hopkins University. Dewey published his own textbook on psychology in 1887, three years before James would publish *The Principles of Psychology*. James was not particularly impressed with Dewey's book, although he had had high expectations for it based on a certain brilliance he had recognized in some of Dewey's earlier papers. One of those papers may have been "The Reflex Arc Concept in Psychology," published in July of 1896, only two months before Gertrude Stein's first article on motor automatism would be published in the same journal. In his article, Dewey illuminates the workings of human reflexes and outlines ideas that would find their full expression in books like *Human Nature and Conduct* (1922) and his masterwork *Experience and Nature* (1925).

The idea that captivated Dewey most was a world that operated as an "affair of affairs." Dewey was a process philosopher who saw reality composed of layer upon layer of automatic sequences, mutual influence, and interaction. Dewey extended the laws of habit beyond the governing human behavior and projected it into the entire universe. Everything from the interaction of atoms, to animal behavior, to the movement of thought and feeling in our own minds, are all part of an inseparable system of automatic processes that trigger each other, moderate and alter each other, sometimes conflict with each other and, in the end, result in everything that is.

Let's start with a situation similar to one Dewey uses to explain the reflex arc concept in his early paper: you see an iron pan with food in it and reach for the handle. The handle is hot when you touch it and your hand recoils. We would say that seeing the food was the stimulus that attracted you to pick up the pan, and the pain that you felt when you touched the pan was the stimulus that triggered your hand to recoil. But Dewey says this simple stimulus/response explanation hides the true depth and complexity of the interconnectedness in this situation; leaving us with a view of life that progresses through a series of jerks and reactions when, in fact, he saw a smooth and continuous process of constant—and very subtle—adjustments and readjustments.

When we walked into the kitchen, we were hungry. We were looking for food. That is why we were attracted to touch the pan. If we had walked into the kitchen thirsty, we might simply have walked to the sink and filled a glass of water without even noticing the pan sitting on the stove. Perhaps we had been sitting in our office working when a pang in our stomach triggered a sequence of thoughts and feelings that led to the conclusion that we were hungry. The emergence of the idea that we were hungry in the mind's eye triggered a muscular sequence that led to our standing up from our chair and walking into the kitchen. Arriving in the kitchen and being hungry initiated a sequence that included scanning recent memory, leading us to remember some food that had been cooked earlier. That memory started a sequence that resulted in us turning our head to look at the stove. The entire event was enacted by one habitual sequence after another, each triggered by the last. We might go from working at our desk to eating in the kitchen without ever consciously being aware of it. This was the kind of unconscious automation of human behavior that William James and Gertrude Stein were studying.

Dewey takes what James and Stein were studying in human beings and expands it to include the entire environment around us. He illustrates that everything involved in a situation like the one just described was itself created through triggered habitual sequences, and those sequences were triggered by other sequences, and so on and so on. Reality is an affair of affairs. A seed is triggered into a process of growth that leads to a tree. The tree triggers a woodcutter's process which leads to the chopping down of the tree. A complex series of affairs leads the tree to become the desk that we were sitting at when we first became hungry. The fact that we had food in a pan was contingent on a host of affairs that led to the development and popular use of pans in the culture in which we live. Each sequence is like a line of dominos. The first one is triggered to fall, and the rest of the line topples, one after another. Life is an unimaginably complex series of dominos that fall over in habitual sequences and trip up other sequences as they go. But not only, as James said, are we almost entirely made up of habitual patterns that unconsciously unfold, but reality itself is entirely, or at least nearly so, an amalgamation of habitual patterns of physic and mental sequences that continually trigger each other in a never-ending complex cascade.

One of the implications of this view, and one that both Dewey and James embraced, is that it eliminates the need for any kind of transcendent soul or ego that makes choices and impacts reality. There is no need to assume that there is any part of us that exists outside of the natural process of life and evolution. There is no self that is not part of the affair of affairs of life. Everything that occurs in reality is the result of the unending interaction of habitual sequences. This view flies in the face of how we are generally conditioned to think. We are customarily taught that we are a person, a being, that makes free choices and acts in the world. But Dewey says that we are not persons acting in the world. Reality is just an affair of affairs; habitual sequences trigger other habitual sequences, and all of the thoughts and perceptions that lead us to so strongly believe that we are an individual entity that acts in the world are themselves just more habitual sequences that end up creating a strong sense of self.

One of Dewey's colleagues, the great sociologist George Herbert Mead, was yet another protégé of William James. Mead didn't describe reality as an affair of affairs, but rather as a "conversation of gestures." Sunlight gestures to the plant that it is time to grow. Rain gestures to the cow that it is time to drink. My words gesture to my friend that I will meet them tomorrow. Reality is a grand conversation of gestures. Each gesture communicates the next step in an unbroken chain of life.

Now, let's look at the way Dewey and Mead imagined that our sense of self was formed in the first place. Babies are born with no idea that they are a person. Then one day, by chance, they smile when their mother calls their name. Seeing the child smile at hearing her name, the mother responds with glee. The behavior of responding to the sound of that name is reinforced. Slowly, other behaviors are reinforced. Eventually, the child learns to say, "my name is Nicole." She learns to say this long before she has any idea what it means to have a name or what that name is referring to. All of the gestures that give us a sense of being someone are learned habits of behavior. Only later, when we have acquired the habit of language, do we learn that we are a person that behaves in certain ways and has a name. Of course, even this learning is simply a set of more subtle and complex habitual sequences. From this perspective, there is no self, no person; there is only a set of conditioned habits of behavior that lead to the idea of being someone and to thinking, feeling, and acting as that person.

This is a difficult perspective to embrace. If you want to see the world the way James, Dewey, Mead, and presumably, Stein, saw it, it will take time. You will need to look at all of the things happening inside and outside of you, and make the effort to see them as sequential patterns of habit. Notice how one thing leads to another, and how that triggers successive steps in a pattern that has long been established. Notice the habitual patterns that are reflected in the way that thoughts and feelings interact in our minds. Notice how it happens in the flow of our behaviors and in the choices we make in the world. And finally, notice how it happens in the things around us. Keep looking and noticing that reality is an affair of affairs—a complex, interconnected, overlapping system of mutually influencing habitual patterns.

Once again, this view may strike you as a bit grim, and yet there remains cause for celebration. Why? Because reality is made up almost entirely of habitual patterns, but not entirely. According to Dewey, there is also the existence of impulse, strong tendencies, and energetic bursts that emerge when the path of habitual patterning has become stuck or disrupted. In these moments, when the smooth and unconscious path forward has been blocked, an energetic impulse bursts through and wakes up a higher level of consciousness. This higher level of consciousness allows for novel responses that can resolve the obstacles blocking the path of the habitual flow of life. These energetic impulses, when experienced by humans, are the source of novelty and genius. Under the influence of these higher impulses, we become an expression of a higher being, our higher Self.

Let's use a simple example of this to illustrate the point: imagine that you get up in the morning and get ready to go to work. You brush your teeth, shower, dress, and have breakfast, all the time barely aware of what you're doing. One habitual sequence enacting itself after another, without the need for any conscious control on your part. Suddenly, as you walk out the door toward your car, you realize that your keys are not in your coat pocket. An impulse shoots through you. Maybe it is frustration or fear that you will be late for work, but however you identify it, it is an energetic impulse that shoots through you and catalyzes a shift into greater consciousness. Your mind starts to expand its purview. Suddenly, you're thinking about the last time you used your keys. You start imaging all of the places you tend to leave them. You walk around the house. A whole new level of affairs has opened up, and this heightened conscious activity will continue until the keys are found and you can relax your consciousness and sink back into the habitual pathways of getting in your car and driving to work.

Now, I want to share a more profound example from my own life. At one time, I was living what most people would consider a good life. I was successful in a good career, married to a wonderful woman, and living in a beautiful house in a great neighborhood. My life was going splendidly, and then I discovered spiritual work. Suddenly, I started to realize that something much bigger was calling me. I studied and explored and did spiritual practices. My new spiritual interests were taking up more and more of my time and energy, and it was creating conflict in my career and with my wife. I was falling out of harmony with the patterns that had been established in my life. The tension escalated to a point of crisis and I made a monumental decision—a decision that remains, to this day, the most unprecedented and truly authentic decision I have ever made. I decided to leave the life I was living, as amicably as possible, and start a new, spiritual life. When I think about it now, this decision seems to stand in direct opposition to everything that had come before. I still don't understand where I found the will and courage to make such a bold move.

The result of making that decision and of revealing it to my wife at the time was catalytic and spectacular. At the moment that I was about to tell my wife of my new plans, I felt the intense force of all the habits of my life pushing against me. Those habits did not want to be broken. I felt a wall of terror building to fence me in. I heard a deafening scream as I opened my mouth to speak. I told my wife that I wanted to live a different life, but the screaming in my ears was so loud that I could not hear the words come out of my mouth. But once they were spoken, something happened. A huge energetic burden fell away from my body. It felt like I had been held in a straitjacket of ideas dictating what I could and couldn't do, and suddenly it was gone. I felt as light as a feather. Emotions that had been pent up inside me were suddenly being released in waves of tears followed by fits of laughter. The strength of the emotional release was more intense than anything I had ever experienced before.

Later that day, I realized that I was free—free of the habitual patterns that had been holding me in place. I was free of all of the ideas about myself, and my life that had guided every decision I had ever made. My mind was open. There was a sense of electric energy surging through my body. I felt consciously aware, with a depth of clarity that I had never experienced before. It was as if I had arrived here in my life for the very first time. I looked back over my history, imagining each major decision in my life, and from this vantage point, it didn't feel like I had been present for any of them. They were not decisions that I had made. They were decisions that had come as the consequence of habitual sequences of thought coupled with conditioned beliefs, expectations, and emotional patterns. I had watched them happen, believing that I was making them, but the belief was just another habitual pattern of thinking.

I had always thought that I was a free thinker. After all, I was a meditator and a spiritual seeker. But now it was clear that I was living exactly the life I had been taught that I should live, complete with a good job, a beautiful wife, a white house with a white picket fence, and two cars in the garage. I had not been living my own life, I had simply been perpetuating the values and norms of the culture as they had been taught to me. But now I was off the cultural conveyer belt. I could see how the social current of learned values keeps moving us forward, shaping each of us in the cultural mold of our time. I looked ahead and I saw that, if I had not stepped off, I would have lived a future that was dictated to me by culture, or what Dewey would have called "a life of colorless conformity (*Human Nature* 16)." Now, I was free. It was exhilarating and terrifying: exhilarating because every door was open, the possible futures I could live were endless, and terrifying because I no longer had a roadmap to guide me. I was beyond the rules of life. I was free to make my own decisions and burdened by the necessity of taking full responsibility for them. I wasn't living according to anyone else's plan. This would be my life from now on.

The deep inner freedom, and the associated expansion of consciousness that awakens when we are thrust out of our habitual patterns of being, offer a tremendous opportunity. Freed from the previous constraints of life, we can create a completely new existence, lived according to a different set of values and concerns that will establish an entirely new set of habitual patterns as a result. And this is how life continually transcends itself. In *Human Nature and Conduct*, Dewey writes, "In the course of time custom becomes intolerable because of what it suppresses and some accident of war or inner catastrophe releases impulses for unrestrained expression" (163). So, when the constraints of life become intolerable, an energetic impulse bursts forth in us and breaks through the invisible walls that bind us. We are catapulted into the wide-open expanse of pure possibility, where the laws of habit immediately go to work establishing new patterns upon which we can stabilize. In time, these new habitual ways of being will themselves become intolerable and another energetic escape will initiate the discovery of a new way of being that will establish itself upon a bed of new habits. And this is how life progresses, continually transcending and reestablishing itself at higher and higher levels.

Now we see the source of excitement that might have been driving Gertrude Stein's interest in exploring the bottom nature of our habits. All her life, Stein was preoccupied with the idea of genius. She saw herself as a genius, she wanted to be surrounded by geniuses, and she wanted to understand what genius was and what gave us access to it. She was passionate about liberating the higher powers of the mind and dedicated her entire life to liberating human genius in herself and those around her. This passion for liberating higher powers was probably at work behind her drive to understand the mechanisms of motor automatism. And as we shall see, this passion continued to inspire her work decades later in Paris, when she became a leading figure in the artistic avant-garde circles there. One of the central aims of the artists and writers around her was to wake people up by creating art that would disrupt their unconscious habits of perception, emotion, and thought. They wanted to liberate the higher powers of the mind, in part, by interrupting the flow of habitual ways of being.

Stein was very likely motivated, even in her years at Radcliffe, by the possibility of liberating the higher powers of the mind. But there was one thing that she was not much interested in and never would be—and, interestingly, it was something that her mentor, William James, was obsessed with.

As we have established, allowing normal human activities to come under the control of unconscious habit liberates the energy of the mind to explore higher possibilities. Both James and Stein were passionate about that, but James was also passionately interested in what the source of those higher powers might be. Throughout his professional career, he spent a great deal of his time exploring what, today, we would call paranormal and psychic phenomena. Meanwhile, Stein appears to have had little to no interest in these matters. In fact, in her original research, she explicitly states that:

> We must leave out at once all the alleged phenomena of spiritualism, as being still under dispute... Ruling these out there remains a small number of cases apparently not fully explained as automatic... where the reactions seem to be rather too intelligent to involve nothing more than habit and memory. (Solomons and Stein 509)

But while Stein seems to have been perfectly able to set questions about spiritualism aside, William James was never able to, and never, in fact, even tried to.

CHAPTER 2

Our Hidden Selves

IF WE SIT IN MEDITATION and remain very, very still, we will make an interesting discovery. We will begin to feel that there is a baseline vibration buzzing through us. We can almost hear it. Initially, it is faint, nearly imperceptible, but as we sit for longer periods of time, it gets louder. It is like the background noise of machinery running in an office. If you work there for many hours every day, you stop noticing it, but if you turn off all of the computers, copy machines, air conditioners, etc., the silence will be deafening. You will suddenly realize how loud the background noise actually was.

We can think of that hum in our own bodies as the background machinery of life running. It's the hum of blood pumping through our veins, of energy running through our cells, and air moving through our lungs. And below all of that, it is simply the humming vibration of energy itself. Like the hum of electricity as it passes through a wire, the life energy that passes through us has a vibration. The French philosopher Henri Bergson, who was well-known to both Gertrude Stein and William James, spoke of this life force energy as the "élan vital."

If we go a step further, we can imagine that the vibration that underlies our life includes both the élan vital that Bergson spoke of and the bottom nature that Gertrude Stein was studying. That means that the foundational vibration of life includes both: 1) a vital force extended to us from the cosmos itself; 2) the energy that is embedded inside all of the personal and cultural habits that have been ingrained in our deepest core. Thinking in these terms, we can imagine that, inside us, the dynamic energy of life has become intertwined with the energetic binds of personal conditioning and social expectation. Disrupting our deeply habitual tendencies might, therefore, be thought of as a way to unleash the more profound energy of élan vital. This liberation of our inner spirit is quite possibly what Gertrude Stein saw as responsible for unleashing the powers of genius in us. And, for William James, this was the key to unlocking the higher potentials inherent in humanity.

William James was the first major American psychologist. In the year 1875, he taught a course called "The Relations between Physiology and Psychology," which was the first psychology course ever offered at Harvard. James would go on to be instrumental in the founding of the psychology department there.

His interest in automatic writing might have originated with some experimentation of his own. It seems that he and his brother Henry— himself a famous novelist—were busy experimenting with nitrous oxide, leading James to publish an essay called, "The Subjective Effects of Nitrous Oxide," in 1882, in a journal called *Mind*. In his essay, James reports observations he made of the effects of nitrous oxide intoxication, and states that he was prompted to experiment with ingesting the gas after reading a pamphlet called "The Anaesthetic Revelation and the Gist of Philosophy."

The pamphlet was a self-published piece written by an amateur philosopher named Benjamin Paul Blood who lived in the small town of Amsterdam, NY. Blood, it appears, mainly expressed his ideas in self-published pamphlets and articles written for some of the newspapers local to him in upstate New York. Years later, James would admit that he had no idea how that original pamphlet had found its way into his hands, but, in 1874, he wrote a review of it for *The Atlantic Monthly*. Blood's pamphlet contains a long essay written to reveal the insurmountable core problem with philosophy, and the means to transcend it.

The ultimate goal of philosophy is to articulate a theory of everything. The philosophical imperative is to explain the nature and essence of reality by coming to the ultimate understanding of the substance and workings of the universe. However, this endeavor, noble and sincere though it may be, is doomed from the start because our understanding of anything must be contained within the rational structures of the human mind, and the human mind cannot hold the truth of everything.

You see, our cognitive understanding is structured by a system based on a fundamental duality, an essential separation that can be expressed most simply as subject vs. object. In other words, our way of thinking and understanding rests on an assumption that someone is understanding something. Yet, the totality of existence can never be expressed in dualistic terms because the totality of existence is a wholeness from which no outside, subjective position exists to view it from. For this reason, try as it might, philosophy is doomed never to succeed in its primary aim. There will never be a place to stand from which to describe everything because any such place would itself be part of everything.

Do not fear, however, because Blood's pamphlet contains more than just the bad news of philosophical futility. Blood found a solution to the problem. The ultimate wholeness of reality cannot be understood because the very nature of understanding is a knowing that stands apart from the thing known, and the ultimate wholeness cannot be separate from that which understands it. Therefore, you can never understand the All of reality, but you can experience it. Blood's great discovery, the tremendous insight that drove him to publish his pamphlet, was that, through the use of nitrous oxide, anyone can experience the ultimate Oneness that Is.

The inhaling of nitrous oxide obliterates the formal structures and categories of our minds. All dualities—subject/object, universal/particular, knower/known, etc.—dissolve into a unitive wholeness that can be experienced directly but never understood. The initial ingestion of nitrous oxide leads to unconsciousness. But, with over fourteen years of experimentation with the drug, Blood discovered that, as you reawaken from your temporary anesthetic slumber, there is a transitional moment when you are consciously aware before the dualistic structures of the mind have reformed. In these revelatory moments, you experience Oneness. You see the unity of All in its full glory.

This possibility drove James to write a review of the pamphlet in which he states that Blood has found a mystical substitute for the answer which philosophy seeks. James elaborates on the anesthetic revelation by quoting from the pamphlet, adding his own capital letters for the line where Blood claims that in coming back to waking consciousness "THE GENIUS OF BEING IS REVEALED" ("Review").

James also refers to the Eastern term "nirvana" in his review. He first asserts that the idea of nirvana has been expressed in so many different forms throughout the history of religion that it must be pointing to something meaningful. Whatever it was that Blood discovered, James believed, was the same thing that the term nirvana is pointing toward. James summarizes Blood's statement that the answer to the great mystery of existence, that feels so impossible to find, can only truly be discovered by rejecting the challenge, because only then do we realize that the answer has always been with us, in the too-easily overlooked immediate experience of the fullness of life. James also asserts that, even if nitrous oxide can deliver us into the experience of unitive wholeness, it is undoubtedly an inferior substitute for the mystical practices that have million-times better credentials ("Review"). Still, James was intrigued enough by "The Anaesthetic Revelation and the Gist of Philosophy" to be inspired to conduct his own experiment with nitrous oxide that he reported on in "The Subjective Effects of Nitrous Oxide" eight years later.

The way James conducted his experiment was simply by inhaling the gas and passing out. He would position himself so he would land on a bed with a desk in front of him. As he woke up, he would grab a pen and write the first words that formed in his mind. In this way, he hoped to capture some wisdom communicated directly from the genius of being. In the first paragraph of his essay in *The Atlantic Monthly*, James states:

> I strongly urge others to repeat the experiment, which with pure gas is short an harmless enough...With me, as with every other person of whom I have heard, the keynote of the experience is the tremendously exciting sense of an intence [sic] metaphysical illumination. Truth lies open to the view in depth beneath depth of almost blinding evidence. The mind sees all the logical relations of being with an apparent subtlety and instantaneity to which its normal consciousness offers no parallel; only as sobriety returns, the feeling of insight fades,

and one is left staring vacantly at a few disjointed words and phrases...("Subjective Effects of Nitrous Oxide")

During his revelatory experiences, he saw the true essence of reality and knew beyond a doubt that perceiving the unbroken and infinite continuity of being is the highest possible attainment. Yet, the words that he would write upon coming back to consciousness would make no sense at all. There truly was no way to bring the enormity of that vision back through the narrow passageway of the conditioned mind.

All of this experimentation occurred very early in James's career. It was 1882 when his report on the effects of nitrous oxide was published, eight years before his masterwork, *The Principles of Psychology*. James, at the time, was a relatively unknown college teacher. It might be easy to dismiss these early writings as youthful explorations, interesting and entertaining, but not particularly significant, except for one thing. The very last essay that James would publish in his lifetime, only one month, in fact, before his passing, was called "A Pluralistic Mystic," and its purpose was to introduce the ideas of Benjamin Paul Blood to a wider audience. At the start of this essay, James speaks about Blood's pamphlet "The Anaesthetic Revelation and the Gist of Philosophy" stating, "I forget how it fell into my hands, but it fascinated me so 'weirdly' that I am conscious of its having been one of the stepping-stones of my thinking ever since" (*Writings 1902-1910* 1295).

The vision that James appears to have found in that short, self-published pamphlet is, in essence, identical to the vision that has inspired me during my entire adult life, right up to the writing of this book. It is a recognition that, behind the apparent reality of separation and division, lies a unitive wholeness that contains an inherent wisdom—the genius of being—that cannot be held by the mind.

Our minds, conditioned as they are to see individual things against a background of space, can never be made to contain a reality that must, by definition, allow for no separation at all. Chopsticks, however adeptly employed, cannot be used to eat broth. Despite our most passionate attempts, the liquid will always slip back into the bowl from which we had hoped to extract it. In the same way, our attempts to explain the inexplicable and describe the indescribable will never bring satisfaction.

Our minds operate according to a representational principle. They are amazingly adept at drawing lines of division that isolate portions of the underlying wholeness of reality and then representing those isolated portions with concepts. Finding ourselves in an infinite, unbroken continuity, we overcome the overwhelming mystery of it all by chopping it up into comprehensible bits. This way of thinking works very well for many things, but the one thing it can never approach is the essential unity behind it all. Conceptual thinking allows us to understand everything, except the original wholeness from which everything came.

James found a reason for hope in Blood's pamphlet because, although the ultimate truth cannot be understood by the mind, it can be experienced. Blood's discovery—and James's subsequent confirmation—that the use of nitrous oxide can reliably reveal the inherent wholeness and genius of being was a cause for celebration. James was skeptical of the means, "What blunts the mind and weakens the will is no full channel for truth," he said ("Review"). Yet, he was heartened that the ultimate truth could be experienced if we found a way to bypass the structures of our conceptual mind. Unleashing "the genius of being" and the hidden potentials that lie behind our conventional perceptions of the world would become the core of James's work.

I resonate so deeply with James's ideas because of my own profound experiences of that inherent wholeness, or cosmic consciousness, especially those I had as a child. These initial visions of the totality of being were soon cut off from me, leaving me, at a tender young age, desperate to liberate myself from the constraining influence of my mind. Having lost access to the cosmic nature of my being, I began a search that would eventually define my entire life. But I would not remember the cosmic experiences that ignited the search for decades.

One of the earliest spiritual explorations that I have always remembered involved me walking through my kitchen one day when I was still a bit shorter than the countertop. I could not have been more than seven years old. Suddenly, I remembered something. Something very important that I had been doing the other day. It was something I did in my father's car, a station wagon which was, at the time, parked in our driveway. I ran out the door and into the car. I climbed into the front seat and sat behind the driver's wheel. I tried to make myself remember what I had been busy doing here.

"Oh yes," I remembered, "I was trying to stop my mind."

I locked the car doors, ready to try again. Then I closed my eyes and concentrated. I saw all the thoughts coming and going. But that was the problem. The thoughts were blocking me from seeing something very important on the other side. I couldn't remember what was so important beyond all the thoughts, but I knew it was out there and I wanted to see it very badly.

With all the intensity of concentration that I could muster, I tried to freeze all the thoughts. I wanted to stop them and dispel them. But try as I might, I couldn't do it. They just kept coming and coming. I would concentrate very hard to try to see behind them, but there was always another thought in the way. It was a constant bombardment. Then it dawned on me: there might be a way.

It was clear that I couldn't stop the thoughts and make them go away, but maybe I could squeeze past them. Since I experienced a never-ending succession of thoughts, one after another, there must be a place where one thought ended and the next one began. If I could pay close enough attention, I reasoned, I could use whatever gap might exist between one thought and the next as an escape route. I could slip between two consecutive thoughts into the mysterious expanse beyond.

But try as I might, I was not able to find a gap. To my surprise, thoughts have no beginning and no end. I kept finding that I would be in the middle of one thought, paying very close attention, waiting patiently for the end to come, and then I would find that I was in the middle of the next thought. I had missed the ending of one and the beginning of the new one. I had simply leaped from one to the next. It was as if, as I was approaching the end of one thought, I fell into a form of waking amnesia, only to regain consciousness in the middle of the next one. I tried so hard to stay consciously awake through the transition, but I couldn't. I always lost awareness just before the critical moment and had to start over again.

I came to the car a number of times after that to try my luck at slipping through thought into the mystery beyond. I have no memory of how many attempts I made after the one incident that I clearly remember, and no memory of how many times I might have tried my daring escape before that. But in the end, I know that I gave up. I became resigned to the grim reality that there was no way out. I was trapped in my mind.

I gave up my childhood attempts to see beyond the mind, but the mystery of what lies beyond thought has been the driving force of my lifelong, spiritual search. Like James, I knew even then that we are a part of something wonderful, something vast and wise beyond words. Over the years, I would pursue that mystery relentlessly, at first as a secondary preoccupation to my ordinary life, but soon as the primary focal point around which my entire life revolved.

Exploring James's excitement around the ideas of Benjamin Paul Blood and the revelatory insights of nitrous oxide gives us a snapshot of the possibility that inspired James's work. But, if we look at an article James published in 1890, called "The Hidden Self," a fuller picture emerges. As the picture of James's inspiration fills out, we see not only what he believed he could discover on the other side of the conceptual mind, but also why he had been so interested in the automatic writing practices that Gertrude Stein had been busy with.

By the year "The Hidden Self" was published in *Scribner's Magazine,* James had been recognized as America's leading psychologist. He had established America's first experimental psychology laboratory at Harvard, and his two-volume masterwork, *The Principles of Psychology,* was published the very same year. In addition to James's more mainstream accomplishments, he had also, by this time, been heavily involved in psychical—or what is better known today as paranormal—research for eight years.

In 1882, while traveling in England, James met a rather eclectic collection of gentlemen who had, only months before, formed the Psychical Research Society. The mid- to late-nineteenth century saw a cultural battle being waged on two fronts. It is well known that science was establishing its dominance and wrestling cultural power away from traditional religious institutions. But there was a third warring party called Spiritualism, the newly formed domain of spiritual, but not religious, belief systems that were focused on mystical, spiritual, and paranormal phenomena. Spiritualists believed that these happenings proved that our souls extended beyond the boundaries of our current bodies and lifetimes.

The Spiritualist movement is said to have begun in the bedroom of the Fox sisters, Maggie and Kate, in a farmhouse in Hydesville, NY—only two and a half hours from Amsterdam, NY, where Benjamin Paul Blood lived. The Fox sisters, sitting in their beds, would hear spirits rapping on the walls and started offering demonstrations of their occult talents, which drew larger and larger crowds and initiated a movement that, at its peak, would attract eight-million followers.

Generally speaking, scientists naturally dismissed the Spiritualism craze as utter nonsense, and James opened "The Hidden Self" with a critique of how unscientifically closed-minded he found this. James describes how each branch of science sees itself as "a closed and completed system of truth" ("Hidden Self"). And yet, all around their accepted beliefs, theories, and facts, there "floats a sort of dust-cloud of exceptional observations..." ("Hidden Self"). This "dust cloud" of contrary facts and observations is ignored by each branch of science in order to maintain an image of itself as holding a complete understanding of its area of study. Most people's minds are so unfree that once they have been indoctrinated into the accepted truth of a scientific discipline, any other possibility becomes unimaginable. "Only the born geniuses let themselves be worried and fascinated by these outstanding exceptions...," James claims ("Hidden Self").

He mentions mystical experiences specifically, describing how occurrences of a mystical nature can be found scattered throughout history. These occurrences are ignored by the scientific community, and yet there has always been a community just as large that explores, practices, and communicates these occurrences from generation to generation. Ignoring such a large body of evidence on the basis that it does not fit well with accepted theory and understanding is radically unscientific. James then proposes to introduce the readers of *Scribner's Magazine* to the newly developed field of "psychical research," and specifically, to the work of Pierre Marie Félix Janet—a pioneering French psychologist who worked with trauma patients and coined the term "dissociation" to describe some of the psychological ailments he treated, although he would later be diagnosed as hysterical himself.

Janet's patients often exhibited severe and inexplicable symptoms including immobilized limbs and loss of the ability to taste. But by using hypnosis, Janet discovered that he was able to bring some of the dissociated functions back to life in a most remarkable way. By putting his patients into states of deep hypnotic trance, he found that alternative personalities would emerge. The first self, Self 1, would have no use of her right arm (Janet's patients were generally women). But when Self 2 would wake up under hypnosis, she would have full use of her right arm. Self 1 would have no knowledge of the existence of Self 2, but Self 2 would know all about Self 1 and was able to state clearly that Self 1 was definitely not her.

Janet also found that, in some instances, he could speak to Self 1 while Self 2 would be able to simultaneously communicate with him in automatic writing. In this way, the doctor found that he could have two conversations at the same time, with two different personalities in the same body.

Janet used the term "subliminal self" to describe this mysterious sub-personality. Sometimes, the good doctor would continue to deepen the trance state and find that yet another self, Self 3, would emerge with a new set of characteristics and capacities. Self 3 would know all about Self 2 and Self 1, but the previous two would know nothing of Self 3.

James was fascinated by Janet's findings. There were—potentially in all of us—hidden selves with characteristics and capacities about which we know nothing. Janet, for his part, concluded that the knowledge and capacities of any submerged self could never exceed the potentials and experiences of the total embodied person. In other words, the subliminal selves might know things that the original self did not know, but they could never know things that the original self couldn't possibly know.

James did not believe this was necessarily the case. He mentions that he knew one non-hysterical woman who was able to know facts about people she had never met, seen, or even heard of before. Undoubtedly, he was speaking of the trance medium Leonora Piper, who he studied extensively in his psychical research and who became a lifelong friend.

How many selves might be buried inside our psyche? And what if those selves extend beyond the limited experience of this lifetime? Perhaps there is no end to the expansion of our selves. The idea of unlocking the latent human potentials of these deeper selves energized James's imagination. His orientation toward psychology was focused less on curing psychological ailments and more on discovering and unlocking our secret inner capacities.

James was far from gullible, although his willingness to courageously take mystical and psychical oddities seriously brought him much derision among some of his peers. Still, James attempted to bring real scientific rigor to his psychical studies, and he uncovered many frauds among the mediums he met. He wasn't advocating for Spiritualism, per se, rather, he wanted to extend the horizons of science to embrace and study the unexplainable. One of the hallmarks of his philosophy would become a fierce insistence that exceptions to the rule could not be ignored. That, he believed, was the only truly scientific attitude to take.

William James had seen the true unbroken continuity of reality. He knew that, ultimately, there was no fixed division that separated us from the rest of the cosmos. He saw our inner world, not only as a personal interior but as the interior of the whole. There was no way to know how far our selves might expand beyond the limited experience of our conscious self, or even of our physical life. James did not want to ignore these magnificent and mysterious realms of being inside us. He felt that it was "of the most urgent importance" that "a comparative study of trances and the sub-conscious states" be established ("Hidden Self"). Although it would be many years before James would publish his mystical masterwork *The Varieties of Religious Experience,* when he finally did, he would find a way to intelligently explore the underlying mechanisms of spiritual awakening and transformation, and pave a road toward the serious exploration of mystical and paranormal experience outside of the established religious traditions.

In 1906, James, now a well-established superstar in the academic worlds of philosophy and psychology, delivered the presidential address of the American Philosophical Association at Columbia University. A year later, he published an essay created from that address called, "The Energies of Men." By that time, the bulk of James's lifetime was behind him, and he wanted to use his celebrity and reputation to legitimize and encourage the exploration of our hidden inner capacities. The message he delivered was meant to set a new course for future research by focusing on the exploration of the profound, secret potentials of humanity. His address was largely ignored by his peers, but the essay was widely reprinted in popular magazines and newspapers. From our vantage point today, we can look back and see that James's essay served to accelerate the movement of American culture in the direction that would give rise to the Human Potential Movement and the East-meets-West spirituality of the later twentieth century.

In the very first paragraph of the essay, James mentions the work of Professor Pierre Janet that he had reported on extensively in "The Hidden Self." James quickly states that he wants to use his address to speak about a topic that is never studied in academia but is of great concern in everyday life, namely, the amount of energy available to us to live our lives. We all know that our level of energy goes up and down all the time, and these ebbs and flows have a dramatic impact on the quality of our life. As he goes on, he makes it clear that his real interest is in the secret reserves of energy and power that lie within us ready to be tapped when needed ("Energies" 322).

We are all familiar with the experience of working to the point of fatigue and then quitting. "But," James says:

> ...if an unusual necessity forces us to press onward, a surprising thing occurs. The fatigue gets worse up to a certain critical point, when gradually or suddenly it passes away, and we are fresher than before. We have evidently tapped a level of new energy, masked until then by the fatigue-obstacle usually obeyed. (323)

James was fascinated by the hidden powers of reserve energy that emerge only when we are pushed beyond our limits. In his essay, he describes "amounts of ease and power that we never dreamed ourselves to own, sources of strength habitually not taxed at all, because habitually we never push through the obstruction, never pass those early critical points" (323). James's biographer, Ralph Barton Perry, sees in this article a thread that runs through the entire canon of James's work. A thread that Perry describes as "the conclusion that exceptional circumstances generate exceptional inner power" (Perry 226).

A large section of the address is devoted to an unnamed friend of James's who, suffering from an unstable nervous system, decided to follow Hatha yoga and the guidance offered by the Hindu sage, Swami Vivekananda ("Energies" 326-327). James explains that the spiritual tradition of Hinduism has a long history of using practices and exercises to unlock the hidden potentials within us and reports that, after a few months of practicing a mixture of asana postures, breathing exercises, and Christian prayer, his friend saw incredibly positive results. In fact, a letter received after ten months "read as if written by a different man, patient and reasonable instead of vehement, self-subordinating instead of imperious" (329).

While our access to profound inner capacities can be gained through the demands of extraordinary circumstances and cultivated through practice and commitment, James reveals that hidden inner potentials can also be ignited by energy-releasing ideas that liberate creative imagination. These inner energies are released during the experience of spiritual transformation.

James concludes his address with a final, impassioned plea to focus our attention on the discovery of the true inner powers within us and the development of the means of access that will unleash these powers. This is the thread that runs through all of James's work. Inside us, miraculous potentials are waiting to be realized. There are means already explored—and others yet to be discovered—that can unleash those potentials, and the realization of these should be a primary focus of psychology, not just in academia, but in the lives of ordinary individuals (331-332).

In fanning the flames of the Human Potential Movement, James was continuing the work of his godfather Ralph Waldo Emerson. Emerson shared his godson's fascination with our hidden inner capacities and our ability to realize them. The following quote, generally attributed to Emerson, communicates a sentiment that James would fully embrace, "What lies behind us and what lies before us are tiny matters compared to what lies within us."

CHAPTER 3

Surfing Higher Dimensional Currents of Being

AT AN EARLY AGE, I lost touch with the cosmic nature of my being. After that, I felt misplaced in the world. Even as a young child, I felt like I didn't belong. It wasn't a particularly painful experience, more odd and disconcerting. I saw what the adults around me were doing, but I didn't understand why it was so important. When I went to school, I wasn't interested in the things the other kids my age cared about, and never had much to say to them. I remember getting on the school bus heading to kindergarten. As the little ones, we would sit in front. When I looked at the back of the bus where the older kids sat, it seemed like everyone had something to say. I couldn't wait until I was older, so I would have something to say too.

But in fourth grade, when I was finally able to sit in the back of the bus, I would look ahead and see that everyone was talking, even the kindergarteners way up in front, and I still had nothing to say. Something was clearly going on that everyone was in on, except me.

By the time I got to high school, I had learned to fit in. I consciously adopted a humorous disposition and made people laugh whenever I could. Inside, I still had no idea what the point was. But there was one thing that I loved: the stars at night. On warm summer nights, I would lay out on the grass and look up into the dark, starlit night. I would think about how big all of those stars were and how far away. Then, I would feel myself laying down on the surface of this spinning planet. As I would contemplate the immensity of the universe, I would start to feel an electric tingling in my back. It felt like energy running up and down my spine that then spread throughout the entire surface of my skin. I could feel it! I could feel how big it all was and the vast context of my life. I was overwhelmed with awe, and wonder, and joy, and bliss. I sat and looked at the stars every chance I had.

I still have these experiences of powerful energy. Sometimes I have it during meditation, other times while just randomly walking down the street. But, most interestingly, I have it when I'm writing or researching a book. When I get interested in something, I get hooked. I start researching, reading this or that, and the larger contours of an idea start to grab hold of me. This reading, and the reference it makes to another book, leads me onward. And sometimes when I start reading something I'm not feeling the energy, but inevitably a new direction opens up; I start reading about something else and the energy comes back. It is the energy of discovery, insight and realization. It feels like falling in love. It is as if I am uncovering something very beautiful and very important. It feels like an idea, but also much more than that. It feels like a being, an entity. It feels like I'm giving birth to something or someone. There are times when the energetic movement is so strong that I have to stop reading or writing because the energy is overwhelming. The ecstasy of discovery is too strong. I can't sit for another moment.

That is what happened to me just now while I was doing research for this book. I was reading *Irresistible Dictation: Gertrude Stein and the Correlations of Writing and Science* by Steven Meyer and I started to realize something about what wants to be said in this book. It has to do with an idea, a mental being that I am giving birth to in this writing. In ways too vague to be certain about, yet too clear to ignore, I felt like I was experiencing the excitement that William James must have felt when he was exploring psychic phenomena, or that Gertrude Stein must have felt in Paris when she discovered the next exquisite piece of art. I feel the two of them coming alive in me, that they have something to say through me.

It became clear to me that this book is about many things and that it is expressing them in multiple dimensions at once. It is about the eternal quest for the ultimate source of wisdom and power that lies within us, but it is also about amazing people like James and Stein who devoted their lives to that quest. In addition, it is about how that power is not simply lying dormant waiting for us to discover it. That power, that higher being, wants to be born, and it is giving birth to itself through us—through me—right now. *It* is writing this book. I am the hand, but it is the author. That is how Gertrude Stein wrote. That is what William James saw in automatic writing. One of the questions that compelled both of them was, 'How is it possible to surrender to something bigger than you and allow it to communicate itself through you?'

I started to write this book because I felt there was something that wanted to be said. I didn't know what that something was when I started, I just felt it energetically wanting to be born. I felt guided to start the book with Gertrude Stein because I was curious about her and I knew of her connection with one of my all-time heroes, William James. From one point of view, the one we've been so deeply conditioned by, I was choosing to write a book and I was choosing to start with Stein. But the opposite of that is equally true—something was compelling me to write it into existence and was showing me how. Something wanted a voice in this world and needed an author to give it one. It chose me.

The story I'm writing is that of writing itself, and the people I'm using to tell that story are gathering for the task. They are coming to me to be written into this account because there is something that wants to be said and they hold a piece of it. I've been fascinated by Gertrude Stein for many years, but only a few months ago did she come into my life with a force that could not be denied. James, my old friend, asked for his place alongside her, and he brought Benjamin Paul Blood and John Dewey along. I am not choosing them, they are volunteering.

Originally, I had intended that this third chapter would be about Ralph Waldo Emerson and his influence on William James. When Ralph Waldo Emerson—who was the godfather of William James—wrote his popular essay "Self-Reliance," the Self that he was asking us to rely on was not our personal self, but the deeper universal Self that is the true source of our being. I felt that, having introduced Stein and James, I wanted to go back and tell you about the work of Emerson that they were building upon.

So, I started reading Emerson to find the material I wanted to share, but it felt flat. It wasn't calling me. I tried to push through it. I went to bed to sleep off the feeling, but it remained in the morning as well. Where had my muse gone? The whole time I was aware of Meyer's book on Stein, sitting on my shelf. Finally, I picked it up. All it took was the preface to unleash the experience of a cascading energetic realization. It said that the title, *Irresistible Dictation,* was a phrase taken from one of Emerson's essays (xix). Of course, it was! Emerson wasn't ready to give up yet; he did have something to say here. That triggered it. My muse was back at work. The energy was flowing again.

The essay that discusses irresistible dictation is called "Fate," and it's part of the writing that Emerson did toward the end of his life. I remembered the essay because I had written about it before. In his youth, Emerson had been a fountain of optimism. He wrote about how we are one with nature—one with a process of evolution whose progress could not be denied. As an older man, Emerson looked back on his life and, although he could see advances and leaps forward, he had to admit that lurking behind every corner was the counterforce of fate, always acting to slow the advance of novelty and change. I remembered reading somewhere that this essay represented a maturing of Emerson's thought, and now it had come to be discussed in Meyer's book, so I looked up the essay to read it anew.

The essay begins by explaining that there are sources of influence acting upon us that are so immense that we cannot see or understand them. I hadn't remembered that, but reading it now sent my energy into a higher pitch; of course, this is the essay that wanted to be included. Emerson goes on to admit that a big part of our lives is destined to be written by forces beyond our comprehension (*Essays and Lectures* 943). To an extent greater than we might want to acknowledge, our lives are guided by an irresistible script written by a hand that we cannot see. This is the hand of fate that works to counter the force of power and personal will within us. Human life is lived in the balance between fate and power.

We naturally want to exercise power through our lives, yet we find ourselves constantly bumping up against limitations. The experience of limitation, Emerson tells us, is how fate reveals herself to us. At gross levels, the experience of limitation is brutish. We want to lift that huge rock, but our muscles cannot bear the weight. But as our soul develops, it encounters limitations that become increasingly more subtle. I want to express love and compassion, and yet I find myself expressing impatience and anger instead. It seems that our own power must constantly contend with the forces of fate that are embedded in the circumstances around us. We appear to be hemmed in by influences that set themselves up against the free expression of our will.

But never fear, as even in this essay Emerson's message is hopeful. Fate is not, in actuality, a force acting against our will. The aims of fate are indifferent to our goals and aims. The sense of limitation does not arise because fate is working against us, but rather because we are working at cross-purposes to fate. As our will extends out, it encounters deeper currents of willful existence. These are the flows of powers that exist all around us that are beyond our ability to comprehend. When our personal will is aimed in directions counter to the aims of these higher powers, they are repelled. When we strike out in opposition to these flows, we are pushed back, sometimes with tremendous force.

But this is not all bad news; in fact, it is to be celebrated, because if we can develop the sensitivity to perceive these deeper flows and align our will with their higher aim, we can become the expression of a tremendous creative power. Our true power rests not within our own capacities, but in the union of our efforts with a universal force. We all experience many impulses toward action, but some of these are impulses of the true heart that originate in a higher part of our being. If we learn to discern these and follow them, the power of the cosmos itself will fuel our actions. We have the opportunity, through the refinement of our spirit, to act as vehicles for the higher powers of the universe. As Emerson poetically puts it, "When a god wishes to ride, any chip or pebble will bud and shoot out winged feet, and serve him for a horse" (*Essays and Lectures* 957).

The experience of co-creative union with a higher source means aligning with the force of what wants to happen. It means letting go of what we think we want, or what we think wants to happen, and embracing the energy of what this moment itself truly wants to bring forth.

When I was trying to write this chapter about Emerson's earlier essays, and his teachings on self-reliance and the over-soul, something was not working. It seemed to me like a good idea, but the energy wasn't there to carry it to fruition. I felt the limitations of an uninspired heart and mind. As much as writing that chapter made sense to me, I couldn't write it. I was thwarted by a force beyond me. That force was the fate, the destiny, of this book.

I could have forced myself to write the chapter I wanted to write and I would have ended up with a different book. It would have been my book, but it would not have been the book that wanted to be written. By waiting for the chapter that wanted to be written to appear, and giving up my plans so that I could align with it, the full power of love and inspiration flowed through me. I had aligned myself with the energy of what wanted to happen, and lo and behold, Emerson did want to be here, but from a different angle than I had thought.

You see, I am not the only one writing this chapter. Yes, it is my hands typing on the keyboard, but there is a great deal more to it than me writing these words. When you align with a universal purpose, the universe conspires to support you—and the universe has a lot of resources at her disposal. You reach out your hand and whatever you need appears in it. The right book calls its attention to you. The right essay finds its way into your life. The perfect idea manifests in your mind. The next conversation you have will fill in a missing piece.

In fact, part of the inspiration for what I am writing now came from a seemingly random exchange of text messages I had yesterday. Of course, the person who I was texting with had no idea that they were playing a part in the writing of this book. They didn't need to know; the universe is perfectly capable of working through us with or without our knowledge of it.

This feeling of universal alignment is one of the greatest experiences I've ever had. It is an experience of inseparable unity with all of creation. You find yourself in constant dialogue with an unknown source of vision and clarity. You become an expression of that higher Self.

This is, indeed, the experience of self-reliance that Emerson wrote about. In "Self-Reliance," one of Emerson's most famous essays, he asks, "What is the aboriginal Self, on which a universal reliance may be grounded?"

(*Essays and Lectures* 268). That source in which we can put complete faith is the source of genius, virtue, and life itself. We discover it through our capacity to act spontaneously, trusting the primary and invisible wisdom of intuition. And in the spontaneous act, the genius of an unknown source reveals itself...

Ahh, our seemingly circuitous route has led us back to where we started: with automatic writing. And yes, it was through the spontaneous act of writing that Gertrude Stein sought to release higher realms of genius.

Writing this way can be exhausting because you are beholden to the energy. When the energy comes, you write. When the energy stops, you wait. Yesterday, I wrote in a flurry of energy. The words just flowed out. Then it was over. The energy stopped. I didn't know what to write next. When that happens, I read and do research, or I just wait. I'm not really looking for information. I'm not hunting for inspiration. I know that, if I wait, the information I need and the inspiration to continue will find me. I keep reading things and letting each one lead me to something else, until a spark flies and the fire of energy returns. I never know what will spark the next flow.

This time, it was a series of text messages I got from a friend who lives in Portugal. I mentioned that I was writing, and she told me that she was too. Much later, she sent me a sample of what she had been working on. The line she sent was this: "I am not a 'poeteer'...the Poetry simply uses me, flowing through the vessel to express itself. The Poetry writes itself."

I read that line and—bang!—there was the energy. What were the chances that we would be writing such similar thoughts at exactly the same time? I felt I had no choice but to accept this as a message from some higher source. I felt the power that was working through the universe to write this book. I surrendered, and the energy of creative realization began to surge again.

Carl Jung called these odd occurrences "synchronicities"—seemingly random events that appear to have a meaningful connection. At one point, in Emerson's essay, he defines fate as "unpenetrated causes" and "a name for facts not yet passed under the fire of thought" (*Essays and Lectures* 948). For Emerson, the word "fate" describes the invisible causes that move life. I believe that, when synchronicities occur, they are revealing some deep underlying process that is moving beyond what we can see. Like the small arc of a huge whale that breaks the surface of the ocean for a moment, synchronicities are evidence of something much larger moving beneath the surface of our perceived reality.

My friend and colleague Jeffrey Kripal of Rice University, writes eloquently of these unseen energies. He describes them as higher dimensional beings that exist beyond our ability to perceive, but which occasionally cross through our three-dimensional reality and reveal some small part of themselves as they pass by, attending to business of their own that we cannot possibly comprehend. In his books, *Authors of the Impossible* and *Mutants and Mystics*, Jeffrey describes these higher dimensional beings as "Super Stories" that run through human history. They affect us. They develop over time. And they attract authors (and, I would want to extend this, to artists of all kinds) to manifest them as works of art in our three-dimensional reality (*Authors of the Impossible* 141). I believe these higher dimensional beings are the deeper hidden selves that James was so fascinated with. They are not ultimately separate from us. We, and they, are different aspects of the same reality. We are all one multi-dimensional being.

If we want to open to the wider reality of who and what we are, we need to let go of the assumption that we exist as a thing separate from a world in the way we've been taught to think about ourselves. You will remember that, for Dewey, reality was an interactive space of mutual influences—an "affair of affairs." For now, let's refer to it as a field of mutual influences. Physically, this includes the influences of matter, and energy, and gravity. Emotionally, there are intentions, joys, and fears. Mentally, there are ideas, and conclusions, and judgments. All of these different strata of reality are involved in the field of mutual influences that ultimately result in the world as we experience it. When looked at in this way, we are not a self-contained and isolated physical person acting in a world that is separate from ourselves. We are an amalgamation of different elements, actions, and perceptions, in a field of mutual influences. The sense that we have of ourselves as a self-contained, separate, and isolated entity is an interpretation that we have drawn about who we are and held on to ever since. What actually exists is a complex interaction of mutual influences within the experience of the present moment. The only reality is a collection of physical sensations, emotions, and mental concepts. There is not necessarily any entity called a person there beyond the idea of it. We have been taught that all of those experiences belong to a person, but that person cannot be found anywhere. There is no guarantee that any such person actually exists.

This was the whole point of Dewey's paper, "The Reflex Arc Concept in Psychology." We believe that there is something called a stimulus and something else called a response, but that distinction is artificial. Intentions and perceptions and movements lead to more intentions, perceptions, and movements. We have learned to draw a line around some of these and label them as the stimulus of a given situation, and then draw another demarcation and call everything inside it the response. But those boundaries, though useful, are not real.

This same artificial drawing of boundaries of convenience is exactly how William James describes our sense of self forming in his 1892 work *Psychology: A Briefer Course:*

> One great splitting of the whole universe into two halves is made by each of us...but we all draw the line of division between them in a different place. When I say that we all call the two halves by the same names, and that those names are *'me'* and *'not-me'* respectively, it will at once be seen what I mean. (*Writings 1878-1899* 172)

The boundary that defines us is arbitrarily constructed. It is useful in many ways, but it does not represent a real division. And we all know it can also be harmful. For instance, we might create a boundary out of the idea that 'I cannot be successful.' We have drawn a division that separates us from success and makes us different from successful people. We all find unhealthy boundaries like these embedded in our sense of self, and part of the work of psychology is to help us rid ourselves of them. These unhelpful self-definitions were formed unconsciously and built up a strong momentum of habit behind them. It takes work to break these habits, but when we do, we find that we are able to be successful, or happy, or whatever else it was that we were lacking. We feel like a different person. We all already know that the boundaries that define us are arbitrary and malleable to some extent. Dewey, James, and many others are merely suggesting that our sense of self might be much more imaginary than we suspect. In fact, they are ultimately calling into question whether any such division between 'me' and 'not me' exists at all.

Of course, this is also the position taken by many of the great spiritual traditions of the East. It is a school of thought referred to as non-duality, which simply means 'not two,' and states that reality is not a collection of parts, but one continuous whole. William James's description of "a world of pure experience" was such a powerful explanation of non-duality that it was adopted by the Zen master Kitarō Nishida and incorporated into the Kyoto School of Buddhism in Japan.

Take a moment to release your preconditioned assumption that reality is a vacuum of empty space filled with separate, material things. Then, allow your inner vision to open up to reality as a field of mutual influences that occur at physical, emotional, and mental levels. They are constantly interacting: physical sensations generating emotional responses that lead to mental conclusions that lead to physical actions. Can you see reality in this way, as a field of mutual influences, rather than a collection of interacting things?

What we perceive as our self is really a confluence of influences that generate a stable conclusion that we exist. That conclusion, that feeling of being someone, perpetuates itself through time, giving us a sense of ongoing existence. This is not a bad thing, but it is not the only truth. Our sense of being someone creates a platform for a host of possibilities that could not happen without it. We perceive through our sense of self, and there is no reason to get rid of it. What we need to do is learn that the sense of self that we have become so strictly wedded to is not the limit of who we are. We are capable of a lot more than what the person we think we are is capable of. Our self is like a surfboard that we ride through existence. And the mysterious synchronicities that we experience along the way give evidence of huge waves in the ocean of being. They hold so much power, but we can learn to surf them. We can synchronize our energies with theirs and ride them to destinations we could never discover without them. Ultimately, if we let go of a strictly solid sense of self, we might realize that we are the waves as much as we are the surfer.

At one level of being, we are persons—defined by bodies and minds that have memories and histories, and make choices. This level of reality is real, but it is not the only reality. The person that we are is one level of reality, but at a different level, that person is only a part of a field of influences that exist at levels beyond our perception. In the invisible expanse of reality beyond our current perception, other self-aware beings swim in mutual influence with us. When we sense these higher beings, we can surrender to them and allow them to manifest through us into our three-dimensional universe. When we do, we bring new energies into our world, and those new energies open up new possibilities for everyone. This is what I mean by higher Self-expression. If this book is about anything, it is about how we can align our sense of self with higher dimensional beings and release the energies and possibilities of those other dimensions into our world. It is possible that, at some ultimate level of reality, all of the influences that occur in all dimensions can be seen as part of one ultimate being, one all-inclusive, divine existence. Perhaps the non-dual whole of existence that William James and Benjamin Paul Blood discovered in their experiences with nitrous oxide was this ultimate higher Self.

As you know, I teach meditation, and when I do, I teach it as a two-stage process. The first stage, or what I call the "first surrender," is a purely passive acceptance of everything. This depth of surrender can reveal to us the ultimate nature of reality—the unitive wholeness that James and Blood described. These experiences leave us certain that we are that wholeness. It relieves us of the burden of any sense that anything could possibly be wrong. It liberates us to let go of all effort. We are all there is and nothing less. For some, it seems, the journey ends there, in the ultimate truth of who we are. They discover it and never come back. That ultimate being radiates through their life. There are others, however, that experience—or at least taste—the ultimate liberation of the highest truth and feel compelled to create. They start a new kind of life here on earth. They have become dramatically untethered from blind adherence to the separate sense of self, yet they continue to surf, now available to illuminate higher possibilities.

The "second surrender" is a surrender to the higher energies that begin to move through us. As our practice of letting go deepens, we inevitably begin to feel universal energies—birth energies—moving us and inviting us into a process of co-creation. We feel ourselves being carried into a current of awakening. It is a feeling that is analogous to finding yourself caught in an ocean current. We feel like we're being swept away. Often the feeling of being swept away scares us. We feel ourselves lifting off, and so we reach back down to grab something—usually a familiar thought or feeling—to hold on to. Out of fear, we pull ourselves to the ground, and then we have to start all over again.

In meditation, I encourage people to experiment with letting go into the higher energies of this second surrender. Once they have let go passively and start to feel themselves being lifted up and carried away by something bigger than themselves, they can learn to let go into that. Maybe they experience a dreaminess that wants to carry them away, or maybe it is a sense of confusion, or simply a sense of spiritual upliftment, excitement, and inspiration. However it appears and begins to move them, the second surrender of meditation is to allow yourself to be moved, to avoid the temptation of reaching back down and pulling yourself to the ground.

It takes a keen and deeply relaxed mind to not be caught in the reflex of holding on when we feel the ground move under our feet. The habitual recoil happens so quickly that it's over before we realize it. But with practice, we can learn to sit, be present, be still—and most importantly— be available to be moved. In this open state, a deep sense of love for the divine fills us, and that is what allows us to overcome the fear that tempts us to hold on when the spirit moves us. I see this as similar to what Gertrude Stein was doing when she learned to allow her hand to write without her.

When I teach meditation, I ask people to begin by not making a problem out of anything that happens, no matter what it is. Simply rest in conscious contentment, and then, if the subtle currents of a higher being begin to move you, simply allow yourself to be moved. Let yourself go. Don't insist on reaching back and holding on. It may be startling to feel yourself move. It may be frightening. It may be exhilarating. You may not be able to believe how lucky you are that a spirit has chosen to carry you into awakening. However it shows up, simply let yourself be moved. Ultimately, the second surrender in meditation is training you to surf the higher dimensions of reality.

I call those of us who are drawn to co-create with cosmic forces "Artists of Possibility." And part of the primary training for Artists of Possibility is how to surrender to higher currents of being when they move you. I believe that the people we've discussed, Gertrude Stein, William James, Benjamin Paul Blood, John Dewey, and Ralph Waldo Emerson—as well as the many people who will undoubtedly join us in the pages ahead— have all, in one way or another, discovered how to let go and merge with higher possibilities. And each of them devoted their entire lives to express those possibilities.

We, as human beings, have access to powers of creative possibility far vaster than we imagine; in fact, far more vast than we *can* imagine. And that's the point! Our current worldview, the paradigm that we live in, needs to be disrupted in order to unleash the full creative genius of life.

It's not a coincidence that Gertrude Stein learned philosophy from William James and then went on to inspire genius as part of the avant-garde in Paris. There is a direct relationship between her willingness to embrace a radically different possibility for how reality works, and her subsequent contribution to art and literature.

This book is aimed at unleashing extraordinary creative powers. It's about the recognition that we have access to sources of wisdom and creativity far beyond what seems possible. In our current paradigm, we are taught to see ourselves as a separate individual who thinks using the faculties inherent in only our own minds and bodies. We are trained to use our minds to solve problems and we have become extraordinarily successful in many ways. At the same time, many of history's most creative individuals tell us that they regularly tap into a source of genius far beyond their own mind. This is what Emerson was teaching the circles around him to do, it was what William James was trying to prove was happening in psychical phenomena, and it was what Gertrude Stein was trying to achieve in her experimental writing. Our capacity for unleashing extraordinary creative potential requires that we liberate ourselves from the limitations of the paradigm we have been enculturated into. We've been trained to imagine that reality exists before we experience it. It is just there, imposing itself upon us. It is inert and unaffected by our experience of it. But in order to unleash our higher creative potentials, we must embrace the possibility that there is no reality before we experience it. Reality is not something that exists separate from us, it emerges into being as we experience it. We are co-creators of reality.

This view of a radically co-created reality has dramatic implications for how we think about everything, and those implications were being examined in the creative endeavors of people like James and Stein. Every Artist of Possibility, in their own way, opened themselves up to a source bigger than themselves. They became a vehicle of creative expression for a higher power, a higher being, or a higher part of themselves. To engage in this supreme act of creativity, they had to grapple with their sense of identity. They had to transcend limitations and surrender to a force they could never fully understand.

My hope is that you, and I, will find our unique ways to unleash the higher creative potentials that lie within us. But in order to do that, we must first liberate our minds from the ontological assumption of being only a physical entity locked in a three-dimensional universe. We must challenge ourselves to imagine that we are much more than that. Embracing the immensity of a higher vision of reality will demand that we question everything, including the very existence of truth.

CHAPTER 4

Beyond the Really Real

IN THE LAST CHAPTER, WE discussed my writing process in terms of surrendering to the creative energies of insight and realization when they arise. That is how I write. Although, to be honest, it doesn't feel like me writing. It feels like the creative energies are writing through me. I also described the feeling of energy running up and down my spine when I am overcome by insight and revelation. I used to summon that same energy looking up at the stars on warm summer nights, and now I seem to be able to attract it when writing and researching. Some of you will have already recognized the energy I am describing as the energy of Kundalini.

Kundalini is discussed in Eastern enlightenment traditions and is said to be the energy of awakening. It exists inside each of us, coiled like a snake at the base of the back. When it awakens, the energy uncoils and springs up through the spine, and ultimately, through the top of the head. I spent twenty years living in a residential spiritual practice community that was largely focused on the attainment of spiritual freedom through the practice of meditation. We were not particularly concerned with the energy of Kundalini, but my lack of interest in it didn't stop it from finding me.

I had been on a silent meditation retreat for about a month when I woke up one night with a pain at the base of my spine. This wasn't just a dull ache, it was an acute, sharp pain. It felt like I had been hit by a hammer. I tried to remember if I had fallen at some point during the day, but I couldn't recall any such instances. I wondered if I could have possibly broken my tailbone just from sitting so much all day. It seemed unlikely that sitting for hours on a cushion could break a bone, but it was the only explanation I had. It hurt so badly that I couldn't lie down anymore, so I got out of bed and started walking around.

I rubbed the spot with my hand, but it didn't help. I paced back and forth hoping to walk off the pain, but it didn't go away. I began to feel a little overwhelmed by how much it hurt. I didn't know what to do and I was starting to feel desperate. Finally, I sat down on the edge of the bed, hoping that might help.

As soon as my bottom sunk into the bed and relaxed, an energetic release occurred. A column of white light shot up from the base of my spine right through the top of my head. It rushed through me with the force of a firehose and a deafening sound. The light was so bright that it burned my eyes. I closed them, but nothing changed. The light appeared to be as much on the inside as it was on the outside. This experience seemed to last only a brief thirty seconds, although, of course, I was not keeping track of time. When it ended, the last of the light shot up through my head and into the sky. I felt exhausted and very relaxed, blissful in fact.

"Holy shit," I said, "I think that was Kundalini."

I had heard of Kundalini before, but to be honest, I had never taken it seriously. In the schools of thought that I was most familiar with, those kinds of energetic openings were generally considered to be a distraction from the real fruits of spiritual freedom and detachment. So, after the experience, I dutifully let it go and moved on with my practice on the retreat. I believe that was a good thing because, over the next month of the retreat, I had a succession of very powerful spiritual experiences, the accumulation of which radically transformed my life.

It just so happens that, about a year later, I came into possession of a book called *Unmasking the Rose* by Dorothy Walters, Ph.D. The book was a firsthand account of Dorothy's Kundalini awakening and, needless to say, I was very open to hearing about it. After reading it, I wrote a short review of the book for a magazine. Dorothy saw the review and wrote a letter thanking me for it, and we kept in contact on and off after that. Some years later, when the spiritual community that I had been a part of fell apart, I contacted Dorothy. In the wake of the loss of my previous community, I found myself thinking about that Kundalini experience and wondering if I had missed something in it.

After a few phone calls with Dorothy, I realized that my spiritual life, and all of the experiences I had after that initial Kundalini opening, could be seen as the unfolding of the energy that had become unleashed in me that night. Dorothy and I have become good friends since then, and I have had the pleasure of publishing three more of her books: two of her poetry collections, and her second book about Kundalini called *Kundalini Wonder*. In that book, Dorothy points out that many of the most creative geniuses—Beethoven, Mozart, Bach, and Picasso, as well Jung, Einstein, Shakespeare, and Dante—claim that their inspiration was driven by a wildly creative energy. "Is such fervent outpouring the result of sublimated Kundalini?" she asks. "Many think so, and indeed there is reason to suspect a connection between Kundalini and creativity" (170).

I too believe that is true, that the awakening energy of Kundalini is our deepest source of creativity. I also believe that the most profoundly creative act that we can engage in is our own awakening to a new way of being or, you could say, the conscious participation in a paradigm shift. A paradigm shift is a supremely creative act because it does not simply change the elements in the world that we see in front of us. It is a shift from the place we see from, and that means a shift in the very ground upon which our perceptions are rooted, that is, our sense of self. I believe that the energy I felt looking up at the summer sky was Kundalini gently making herself known to me. I believe the energy of Kundalini is the energy illuminating the path that this book wants to take. I also believe, like Jeffrey Kripal does, that the energy of Kundalini can be seen as the energy of a higher dimensional being that I have come into contact with.

I was delighted to discover recently that Jeffrey, who is not only the author of *Mutants and Mystics* but my friend, had described his own energetic awakening experience in his book in ways that are congruent with many of the ways that I have come to see such things:

> My vibrating body felt as if I had stuck a fork in a wall socket... Perhaps more significantly, my brain felt as if it had suddenly hooked up to some sort of occult Internet and that billions of bits of information were being downloaded into its neural net. Or better, it felt as if my entire being was being reprogrammed

65

or rewired. (*Mutants and Mystics* 6)

He goes on to explain:

> It is almost as if some kind of direct, right-brained, mind-to-mind transmission took place, as if those residual plasmic energies were encoded with ideas or structures that could not be 'languaged' but could be stored and later intuited and consciously shaped in the mirror of other resonant or echoing authors until they could appear, now through the prism of the left brain's words, as my books. (8)

In subsequent phone conversations that I had with him, Jeffrey shared his belief that these energetic experiences might best be understood as encounters with other beings—beings more vast than we can imagine. For the duration of time that the incredible energy was burning through him, Kripal told me that he could easily believe that he had come into direct contact with an intelligent being and that his nervous system had temporarily fused with that of a higher intelligence. He was, effectively, being downloaded with massive amounts of information.

Dorothy Walters also speaks of the energy of Kundalini as a being, and during some of my phone calls with her, she even suggested that I speak to the energy when it arose. I tried doing so, and to be honest, the energy did seem to listen and communicate back to me in mysterious ways. Like Jeffrey and Dorothy, I also believe that our spiritual experiences and energetic awakenings can be understood as encounters with higher dimensional beings. I also know that within the materialistic biases of our scientific worldview, there is no way for this to sound anything but a bit crazy, or at least hopelessly speculative, except of course to those who have had such experiences themselves. One of the central pillars of our modern understanding of reality is the separation between mind and matter. This fundamental duality was inserted into the core of our mental framework when the French philosopher, René Descartes, made the distinction between "res extensa," extended and unthinking things, and "res cogitans," unextended and thinking things. Today, we often think of this distinction as material things vs. mental things. If I were to express the same distinction as mental things and real things, most people wouldn't bat an eye. But that, in and of itself, reveals our materialistic bias. Very few would come rushing to the defense of imagined things to insist that they are also real things.

The defense of the reality of imagination is a central tenet of the philosophy that William James worked on his entire life but never felt that he had completed to his satisfaction. He called his philosophy "radical empiricism," and simply stated, it says that all experienced things, including all of the ideas and feelings that describe and relate tangible things—ideas like above, away, before, etc.—must all be considered real things (*Writings 1902-1910* 1159-1161). Nothing that is experienced should be considered unreal. James's psychical research can be seen as a natural outgrowth of this philosophical attitude, and of course, this philosophical attitude could have been equally likely to have grown out of his research into psychical phenomena.

Many mediums and psychics in James's time were fakes, motivated by a desire for fame and money. For that reason, the bread and butter, so to speak, of James's psychical research involved debunking mediums and frauds, although he found that part of the work tedious and boring. Still, he asserted that even if there is just one authentic experience of the paranormal, it has as much claim to be considered a real thing as does the back of your hand.

Gertrude Stein may not have shared James's warmth for spiritualism, but she was deeply steeped in radical empiricism. What makes radical empiricism so radical is how far it extends beyond the original conception of empiricism. Empiricism is the philosophy that tells us that only what we experience can be considered to be real. Radical empiricism goes further by stating that nothing that is experienced can be dismissed as unreal. One of the effects of this philosophy is that it holds our minds open and compels us to look around the edges of accepted facts.

Today, very few people in academic circles would ever claim to be strict dualists in the Cartesian sense. In fact, the idea that our minds are entirely separate from our bodies is generally shunned today in most circles. Of course, that doesn't mean that the line that separates mind from matter doesn't continue to dominate most of our everyday thinking even if few people would admit to it. One of the reasons that Cartesian dualism has fallen so far out of favor is that it presents us with the unavoidable and impossible problem: having to explain how the thoughts in our heads can affect the movements of our bodies.

How can a thought move a muscle if the two are completely separate? How does a mental concept pull on the fleshy fibers and spur them to action? Where is the point of contact between them? Even Descartes found this problematic but decided in the end that it must happen in the pineal gland—perhaps because no one knew exactly what the pineal gland did, and this at least gave it a function.

Cartesian dualism splits mind and matter, thoughts from things. And because we live in a materialistically biased culture, we tend to think of material things as real, and the thoughts and feelings of the mind as secondary, and somehow less real, or perhaps only subjectively real. Taking this assumption one step further, we are taught that the words we use in writing and speech are merely labels stuck on real things and by "real" we mean materially real or tangible.

When I say that I believe that my creative bursts are caused by Kundalini, you will assume that I mean to say that there is a real thing called Kundalini. Of course, in our culture, that means a physically evident thing that can be observed and measured. My statement about Kundalini is seen as a statement of fact, and if you haven't had a similar experience yourself, you will feel justified in calling upon me to prove that such a fact as Kundalini exists. On top of all that, I am saying that the energetic releases that I experience, and that inspire my writing, are encounters with intelligent beings of higher dimensionality that want to write through me. You will naturally assume that I believe that there are real beings somewhere, meaning material beings either physical or energetic, that I am in contact with. Once again, you will rightly expect me to prove my claim.

However, I will not try to prove that Kundalini is real in this sense, or that it is the source of my creativity, or that there are higher dimensional beings that can act through us in extraordinarily creative ways. This book is an attempt to inspire you to be open to that possibility, but if I attempt to prove those things, I will inevitably fall into a trap, because I will have to explain them in terms of the current paradigm. I will be taking my anomalous experiences and attempting to fit them into our customary understanding of reality. What this ultimately means is that I will be trying to validate my beliefs by proving that they do not essentially conflict with our accepted view of reality. But the problem is that they *do* conflict with our current view of reality; they are anomalies, they are part of "the dust cloud of exceptional observations" that James talked about ("Hidden Self"). I would never be able to prove that they are true by showing that they do not present a fundamental challenge to our entire view of reality, because they do. Instead, I will attempt to deconstruct the assumption that facts are only true if they correspond to some pre-existing reality. In fact, I will attempt to convince you to give up the notion of any pre-existing reality altogether. What I need to do, rather than prove that my statements are true in the accepted sense, is to introduce an alternative approach to the whole idea of truth in the first place.

I am not suggesting that we come to a new mutual understanding of what is real and true. I am not trying to convince you that I am right about the things I believe in. What I want to do, instead, is to question what it is that we think we mean when we use words like "reality" and "truth." The late-twentieth-century American philosopher, Richard Rorty, devoted a great deal of his illustrious, though controversial, career to this investigation, and you can find no better overview of his ideas than in his little book, *Philosophy as Poetry*. The title already says so much about Rorty's views and sets up the perfect jumping-off point for our investigation.

Western philosophy has defined itself, since the time of Plato, as an attempt to gain access to reality. In other words, we know that reality is out there, and we want to know what it is. Rorty points out that, wrapped up in this view, is another primary split in our way of thinking: the split between appearance and reality. We know that things appear to us a certain way, and we also know that the way they appear is not necessarily the way they are. Plato's philosophy was aimed at discovering what was "really real." He wanted to use the mind to see through our illusions until we came to the actuality underneath.

This view of reality is the one that we are all steeped in. It is rooted in the assumption that there is something really real underneath all of our perceptions of reality and our claims about truth. It further implies that our perceptions of reality, and our claims about truth, are separate from what is real—they are hanging outside of reality, in some immaterial realm, that doesn't count. When we say that something is true, we are claiming to be pointing from some mysterious outside and objective vantage point toward something that is really real. Within this framework, when I say that I believe Kundalini is the source of my creativity, I am saying that Kundalini is really real and it is the source of my creativity in some demonstrable way. I am making a statement of fact, i.e., a statement that corresponds to a reality beyond it.

This understanding of reality assumes that there is something that exists independent of the way we think about and describe it. Reality is just sitting there, separate from us, waiting to be discovered and described. Knowledge progresses as our ideas become increasingly accurate descriptions of what was there before they were formed. The goal of philosophy is to facilitate human progress, and human progress occurs as we formulate increasingly accurate ideas about reality. This is the view of empiricism because empiricists demand that philosophy must refer to facts of experience. We cannot just make up ideas in our heads and call them true, no matter how much logical sense they might make. We are beholden to develop ideas that can be shown to correspond to what is really real, which boils down to things that we can hear, see, smell, taste, and touch, because our physical senses are the only tool we have to access reality. For those who are interested in such things, this marriage of reality with our ability to perceive through our five senses is actually moving us away from Plato and toward his most famous disciple, Aristotle.

Rorty points out that there are philosophers who oppose this view, himself included. He calls these people anti-empiricists and includes among them Friedrich Nietzsche, Ludwig Wittgenstein, and Ralph Waldo Emerson. These philosophers did not see human progress as a matter of formulating increasingly accurate ideas about reality. They defined human progress in terms of the growth, transformation, and expansion of how we see ourselves and the world. These thinkers did not see reality as something that exists before we do. For them, there is not a reality that was there all along just waiting to be discovered. Reality is not a thing; it is a being and it grows. We are not separate from that being. We are part of reality, and it grows and changes as we do because our growth in understanding the universe is an inseparable part of the growth of the universe itself. All of these thinkers saw imagination, not rational deduction, as the most important human capacity.

These two views of reality are vastly different. The second view was the center of the Romantic Revolution and was developed by thinkers like Emerson and passed on from there. The first view represents the views of Plato, and even more so Aristotle, and it became the foundation of the European Enlightenment and the scientific worldview.

Let's take a moment to think here and understand the difference. If there is a really real underlying reality, beneath all of our ideas and perceptions of it, then that pre-existing reality is the limit of what is possible. We live in a reality that starts with only so much possibility and cannot be expanded. Everything that is possible is there from the start, waiting to be discovered. This allows us to feel safely confined within a fixed reality.

But philosophers like Nietzsche, Wittgenstein, Emerson, and James, would not accept such limitations. They saw an unbounded reality of possibilities with human imagination as the only boundary to reality. The creative work of philosophy is not to discover what is already present and to describe it accurately; philosophy's true role is to create narratives that describe and unlock new possibilities. When these narratives are powerful and imaginative enough, they attract people to live in them. Plato's vision of a really real reality that our words describe, was so powerful that we have been living inside it ever since—not because he accurately described what was already true, but because he narrated a possibility that was so compelling that it became the center of human life for thousands of years. And now, so many of us have been living in that vision for so long that it feels like reality to us.

Rorty saw philosophy as a form of poetry, and there may be a part of us that thinks this is ridiculous. You can't just make something up and make it real just by getting enough people to adopt it. Even if everyone in the world believed something was true, it could still be wrong. You might argue that, at one time, everyone thought the earth was flat, but it wasn't. It was always round, even before we realized that it was. But two retorts immediately come to my mind for this last example.

The first response is to say, "Yes, of course, the world was still round even when we thought it was flat, but that is only true if we define reality in a materialistic sense." If we say that reality is defined by physical stuff, then it makes sense to say that, in reality, the world was always round even when we thought it was flat. But, what if we don't define reality as a physical place?

Instead, I want to define reality as a range of possibilities. Reality is not defined by material stuff, but by what is possible. If the story is true, then Christopher Columbus didn't believe the earth was flat, he believed it was round, and because of that it was possible for him to imagine sailing around it. It would never occur to someone who believed the earth was flat to try to sail around it, and even if such a crazy notion did occur to them, they would dismiss it. If we define reality in terms of what is possible, we could say that, in one important sense, Columbus lived in a different reality than most of the people around him.

The second response would be to explore how deeply co-creative reality actually is. It is not too difficult for us to believe that certain layers of reality are co-creative. We know that money is a created reality that has no meaning outside of human financial systems and agreements. The paper in my wallet is not really worth anything unless someone who understands and trusts the financial system is willing to accept it in exchange for goods. Money is a human invention and it is only money to the extent that we agree to recognize it as such. Something like money, then, is sometimes referred to as a "social reality." Of course, for these same reasons, we also don't see money as really real in the sense that gravity is really real, or matter is really real.

Interestingly enough, Rorty uses the example of gravity in *Philosophy as Poetry* and in his earlier book, *Contingency, Irony and Solidarity.* Rorty didn't want to say that Sir Isaac Newton discovered gravity. Instead, Rorty says that Newton convinced everyone that something called gravity existed and inspired them to talk as if it did. He made up a story about gravity that was so compelling that everyone started talking about reality in terms of gravity and, eventually, it became part of how people experienced the world. Science is poetry too!

"Wait one minute!" you might say. "Money is one thing, but gravity? Gravity isn't something Newton just made up. Gravity is a real thing. It was there before Newton discovered it. Things had been falling down since the beginning of time. Newton was just describing a pre-existing phenomenon and giving it a name."

I understand that this anti-empiricist point of view can be hard to swallow, but let's go slowly. Was gravity really there before Newton convinced everyone that it was? Is gravity even there now? Newton described gravity as a force that acts between physical bodies, pulling them towards each other. He also imagined that some intelligent agent must be mediating that force because it is impossible for things to act on one another from a distance. "Gravity must be caused by an agent," Newton said ("Four Letters"). And elsewhere he added, "I am compelled to ascribe ye Frame of this System to an intelligent agent" (Cahn 10).

A few hundred years later, Albert Einstein envisioned gravity as a distortion of space and time and revolutionized modern physics. Was Newton wrong about gravity being a force? Is Einstein right? An empiricist would say that gravity was always gravity and that Einstein discovered things about it that Newton didn't know. Einstein brought us closer to the really real truth about gravity. But, how do we know what is true? How do we know we are moving closer to the truth about reality if we don't know what that truth is? So yes, things were falling down before Newton—or at least it seems reasonable to assume that they were. The phenomenon of falling bodies was always real, but the story explaining why and how they fall is invented. It is a story.

"Now hold on!" you might say. "You're a nihilist, you don't believe that anything is real and true."

That was a complaint that Rorty had to constantly contend with. But Rorty was not a nihilist. He was something else. He did not believe that we can ever assume that we know what the truth is, where a nihilist is certain that they know the truth. They know beyond doubt that life is meaningless. Rorty wasn't trying to create a narrative to get us to believe that there is no truth, he wanted to create a narrative to convince us that the idea that there is a truth, and the related notion that something is really real, are simply not useful ways to think. If Rorty was anything, he was agnostic. He didn't know what the truth was and he didn't think it was helpful to worry about it; in fact, he thought it was detrimental. This was the same position that William James warned of when he said:

> Each one of our various ologies seems to offer a definite head of classification for every possible phenomenon of the sort which it professes to cover; and, so far from free is most men's fancy, that when a consistent and organized scheme of this sort has once been comprehended and assimilated, a different scheme is unimaginable. No alternative, whether to whole or parts, can any longer be conceived as possible. ("The Hidden Self")

The danger of a worldview anchored in the conviction that, underneath all of our understandings about reality, there is some ultimate and undeniable really real truth is that, once we believe we have found that truth, we too easily end up stuck in our current perception of reality, unable to imagine anything beyond it. What we are talking about here could also be described in terms of paradigm-shifting. A paradigm is the underlying set of assumptions, beliefs, and behavioral practices that create the background upon which we make meaning about the things we see in the foreground. For example, I cannot understand that this item in front of me is red unless I have a pre-existing understanding of color. I can't recognize a fire truck unless I already know what a fire truck is.

The concept of paradigms was explored deeply in the 1962 book *The Structure of Scientific Revolutions* by the historian of science, Thomas Kuhn. In his groundbreaking work, Khun uses the history of science to extract a theory of paradigms, how they work, and how they shift. He also makes a distinction between normal science and revolutionary science. Normal science is the everyday work that scientists do to explain and expand our understanding of the current paradigm. Normal science works comfortably within the framework of the current paradigm, using its background set of assumptions to understand more and more things.

Revolutionary science occurs when the validity of the current paradigm has been called into question. That either means: 1) something has been discovered that should not be possible; 2) some ongoing problem proves impossible to solve; 3) someone simply makes an ingenious leap in logic that leads them to question the foundations of accepted reality. Normal science extends what we know about things that already exist. Revolutionary science changes the way we understand reality itself.

My favorite paradigm-shifting anecdote that I have heard attributed to Ludwig Wittgenstein, although I have never been able to confirm that, is a simple story that goes like this. Wittgenstein asks one of his students, "Why do you think that, for so long, almost everyone thought that the sun circled around the earth, when the earth is, in fact, rotating?" The student answered, "Because it just looks that way." To which Wittgenstein responded: "Really? What would it look like if the Earth were rotating?"

Of course, the punchline is that the world looks exactly the same in either case. What changes with a paradigm shift is not *what* you see, but *how* you see it. To paraphrase some of Kuhn's ideas we could say that when a paradigm shifts, nothing changes but everything is different (Kuhn 111).

We are taught, and generally believe, that we are seeing reality the way reality is, but we are not. We are seeing reality according to perceptual habits that appear spontaneously in front of our mind's eye. A great deal of what we believe to be true, we only believe because it *looks that way*. But thinkers like William James and Gertrude Stein were not satisfied with that. They understood that our experience of reality is bordered by limiting ideas and mental habits. We are trained to perceive and to think in certain ways and not others. But James always encouraged Stein to keep her mind open.

We live inside a paradigm that sees reality as an expanse of empty space, stretching infinitely in three directions and filled with material things that are acted upon by forces such as electricity, magnetism, gravity, and nuclear forces. This is what we typically call "the universe," and the acquisition of knowledge is assumed to be the acquisition of a deeper and deeper understanding of the things that exist in this universe and how they interact with each other. William James wanted to question our whole assumption about the universe. Like many of the philosophers that Rorty wrote about, James, was an anti-empiricist. He, as we have already seen, did not negate the empiricist assertion that all knowledge should be grounded in our actual experience. He didn't believe that empiricists were wrong about that, but that they hadn't gone far enough. Traditional empiricism fits comfortably in the current paradigm. The universe of empty space occupied by things is the container and within that container we have experiences of things and how they interact. An empiricist would say that all of our knowledge and understanding should be drawn from those experiences.

One of the things that James's radical empiricism would not accept was that there was a universal background that was itself not just another experience. What made James's empiricism "radical" was the fact that he believed that all of reality was made up of experiences. There is no physical container within which experiences take place. We live, in his words, in "a world of pure experience" (*Writings 1902-1910* 1159).

In 1904, James published two papers that outlined his understanding of a world of pure experience. The first of these papers was called "Does Consciousness Exist?," a question to which his answer was basically, "No, it doesn't" (1141-1158). James was not questioning the fact of experience, but rather the idea that those experiences happen to someone in a medium called consciousness. You see, in conceptualizing our inner world of thought and feeling, we apply the same model that we use to understand the outer universe. We imagine that, inside us, there is an expanse of inner space that we call consciousness, and that all of our conscious experiences happen in that space. We essentially end up with a model of inner space populated by mental objects that corresponds to our experience of outer space populated by material objects.

James said that there is no such inner space. There are just experiences that are part of a continuous stream of presentation. One experience presents itself, and then another, and then another, and so on. Consciousness is not an inner space filled with mental objects, it is a continuous stream of experiences. There is no reality outside of that stream of experiences. The stream of consciousness isn't happening inside of anything else. Reality is that stream. Reality is a succession of experiences that come in many forms, having different properties. Based on this succession of experiences we create ideas about ourselves and the world, but these ideas are themselves just more experiences that appear in the stream of consciousness. I may experience a belief in a universe of empty space filled with things, but that belief is just another experience, containing no more actual physical space than any other experience. Space is not a real physical thing; space is an idea that shapes and orders other ideas until they create a stubborn habit that feels like physical space. The habit of feeling that space exists continually reaffirms our belief in the actuality of it until there is no way to move beyond it. But our felt experience of physical space, and our conviction in the truth of it, are themselves just other experiences in the unending stream.

In 1882, during a visit to Prague, James met the Austrian physicist and philosopher Ernst Mach and found in him a true kindred spirit in radical empiricism. James and Mach spent a glorious four hours together, undoubtedly discussing some of the ideas that Mach would publish four years later in a book called, *The Analysis of Sensations and the Relation of the Physical to the Psychical,* which essentially spells out his version of James's radical empiricism.

Early on in the book, Mach illustrates our powerful tendency to fill out our partial experiences so that we see wholeness and consistency where none actually exists. I have a desk and it gets painted, but I still perceive it as the same desk. Every day, I experience myself having different moods and different amounts of energy, but I assume that there is one *me* feeling it all. This is because we have been conditioned by the assumption of a split between appearance and reality. We think there is a real desk that is separate from whatever color it happens to be. We think there is a real me separate from how I might feel at any given time.

Let's try a thought experiment modeled on Mach's line of reasoning. You have a desk and then one of its legs breaks. It is still your desk, but now it has to be propped up on a box. Later, another leg breaks and you need another box. The drawers fall apart and cannot be repaired. It is still your desk, but now it is unusable. At what point does it cease to be your desk? At what point does it cease to be a desk at all? Where is this thing I call my desk that I thought existed independent of its appearance?

He applies the same logic to ourselves. We assume that there is someone that exists, an ego, that is us. But where is it? My body continuously grows, my ideas change, I create new memories, and forget old ones. If I think of myself twenty years ago, that person seems like a completely different person than who I am today, but I still cling to the idea that there is only one of me.

Mach's point is that we construct a world of stable things and then we live in it, when in fact, reality—as far as we can know—is nothing but an unending succession of sensations that are changing all the time. The sensations from which we construct our experience of the world fall into three types: sensations of the world, sensations of our body, and sensations of our mind. But the all-important fact is that, in the end, they are all sensations. There is no inside and no outside, no self and no other, there are just sensations. Everything else is interpretation, and our interpretations, over time, begin to feel like something. They become experiences that feel like more than just interpretations; they feel like reality. We live in a world of pure sensation, or to use James's terminology, of "pure experience." Our senses don't experience things as they are. Our senses have been conditioned to experience what we believe is there.

Let's go back to Wittgenstein's unfortunate student who said that "it just looks like" the sun is moving. We have all witnessed the sun's appearance on the horizon at dawn, and yes, it does look like it is rising. But why does it appear that way? Because our perception has been shaped by our belief. We call that beautiful morning event a "sunrise." Everyone we know calls it a sunrise. On the evening news, they tell us what time the sun will "rise" the next morning. Over and over again, the idea that the sun moves is reinforced. And so, naturally, when we go out in the morning, it *looks like* the sun is rising over the horizon and into the sky, but only because we've been hypnotized into seeing it that way.

Instead, try this. Go out one morning, and as the sun begins to appear on the horizon, imagine that you are on a huge sphere that is slowly revolving forward. Allow yourself to become very conscious of the fact that the apparent motion of the sun rising into the sky is actually caused by your gently rolling forward on the surface of the earth. Keep concentrating on this interpretation of the scene in front of you and you will eventually start to feel yourself rolling forward. Our seemingly spontaneous physical sensations of life can actually be conditioned experiences based on our ideas about reality. How many of the things that "just feel like" they do, feel that way only because that is how we have been conditioned to feel them? It is not only our thoughts and emotions that are shaped by how we think; even our immediate physical sensibilities are shaped by assumptions and beliefs.

Ernst Mach believed that it was safest to assume that our understanding and perceptions of reality were merely one abstraction after another, all the way down to the most basic and obvious aspects of the universe. Mach didn't even believe that anything called matter actually existed— and he was a physicist, and a really good one. We experience objects and then we are taught that those objects are made of a substance called "matter." But Mach thought that the idea of matter was just that, an idea. It was a concept that might be a convenient—and even useful—way to think, but it wasn't necessarily real. In fact, in defining it, he said that "... matter must be regarded as a highly natural, unconsciously constructed mental symbol for a relatively stable complex of sensational elements..." (Mach 311). Matter is not an actual substance, it is an idea, a symbol used to signify a set of experiences that remain relatively stable over time and that we have learned to experience as if it exists.

Mach admitted that the human endeavor of science had achieved amazing results. But, the downside of this success was that it created an almost irresistible temptation to believe that scientific speculations about reality are true, in the really real sense. Mach saw how easy it is to believe that what scientists tell us is true, especially if they all agree. He also saw that it is just as easy for scientists to assume that their own theories are true. This was something Mach wanted to avoid. Our mental models should not be confused with descriptions of reality. When scientists talk about their models of reality as if they are descriptions of what is actually real, they are engaging in metaphysics, not science. Like James, Mach saw that the world we actually live in is a mental construct created out of interpreted impressions. The work of science is not to tell us what reality really looks like. The job of science is to look for patterns of experience that can be understood, replicated, and ultimately utilized in the service of a better future. Tying ourselves down to beliefs about what is really real just slows us down. It makes us reluctant to let go of what we believe when faced with conflicting data. When we think we know what is really real, we feel secure and tend to defend what we think we know, even in the face of contradictory evidence.

The reality we live in is an interpretation drawn from sensuous experiences, and we have no way of knowing how much of what seems to be rock-solid-real is actually just very deeply conditioned habits of perception. To put it another way: we live inside of a paradigm, a set of assumptions about what is real. The paradigm manifests itself in society in the things that people believe in, the ways we talk, and what we do. The dominant paradigm of a culture is constantly reinforcing itself and strengthening its hold on the minds of everyone within that culture. Eventually, the assumptions of the dominant paradigm simply become the obvious truth to everyone: "Of course the sun goes around the earth! Just look and see. Doesn't it look that way to you?"

When contrary evidence is introduced, it is hard to take it seriously, and the only way to do so is to force it to prove itself in light of what we already know to be true. Of course, if the evidence is contrary, there will be no way to prove it. I once saw a television special that presented itself as a panel discussion. The panel featured three well-known thinkers who fell squarely in the scientific materialist camp. The fourth panelist was an even better-known New Age spiritual teacher. What ensued was more or less a three-on-one ambush. Over and over again, the three materialists would demand that the spiritualist prove that the universe was made of consciousness and not matter. And over and over again, the spiritualist would take the bait and try to explain his spiritual position in material terms. And over and over again, he would fail. The whole time I was hoping that he would turn the tables and demand that the others prove that matter existed, but he never did. After a while, I couldn't watch anymore.

According to Richard Rorty, when worldviews or paradigms compete, one doesn't triumph over the other by winning an argument and proving that it is more real. The paradigm that prevails will do so because it captures more human imagination and brings more people into its narrative. It does not necessarily succeed because it is right, but because it is more compelling.

So, I am not going to try to prove that Kundalini is real, or that it is the true source of creativity, or that higher dimensional beings exist and can emerge through us, at least not in any material sense. I don't know if any of those things are true. But I don't know if matter exists either. What I know is that I have had experiences—some dramatic, some more subtle—of a profound energy running through me. Those experiences match other descriptions of Kundalini that I have read in Eastern spiritual literature and from modern spiritual practitioners. I also know that when I am feeling that energy, I appear to have insights and realizations that lead to spoken and written expressions that amaze me. I hear myself speaking, or see what I have just written, and I don't feel like it came from me. It feels like it came through me from a source bigger than me. Wherever it comes from, it is much better than anything I could say or write. I know that when that energy flows, I feel like I approach my highest creative potential. That's what I know. Anything beyond that would be speculation and metaphysics. It might be useful speculation and metaphysics, but it would not necessarily be true in the really real sense.

My suggestion is that you read this book without worrying about whether what you are encountering is true or not, and see where it takes you. If, in the end, we do live in a reality that is indifferent to the way we think about it—if, in fact, reality was here before you started reading this book, and will be there, exactly the same in the end no matter what you read about—then nothing will change, anyway.

But personally, I don't believe that. I believe that the reality that you participate in creating after reading this book could become a different reality than the one you were in before reading it. And in this new reality, you could become an Artist of Possibility, meaning someone who consciously participates in the creation of a new reality.

CHAPTER 5

Sharing from the Continuous Present

I INTRODUCE RADICAL EMPIRICISM IN this book for two important reasons, and I want to be completely clear that neither of those reasons is to convince you to believe that it represents the really real truth about reality. One reason is that they represent a radically different interpretation of reality, and the light cast by that alternative can illuminate some of our most deeply held assumptions. The second reason is that this philosophy was well-known to Gertrude Stein and shaped many of the ideas about writing and creative genius that we will explore in her work, and that of other Artists of Possibility.

All of these explorations are in service of unleashing our true co-creative potentials. To do that, we must find a way to liberate ourselves from any assumption of separation from the world, recognize the true depth of mutual influence that exists between us and the cosmos, and finally, learn how to allow higher orders of creativity to flow through us. In a sense, what we think about those higher creative energies, and where we imagine they come from, is only important to the extent that those ideas allow the energies to flow through us. It doesn't matter if our ideas about creative genius are accurate in the factual sense. What matters is that more of us gain access to our higher creative powers, and changing how we think about ourselves and reality might be the key to realizing our full potential. One of the things we are exploring together is the depth to which what we think about reality shapes reality. We are musing over the degree to which what we think is possible creates what's possible. The way we are currently taught to think about reality and ourselves makes some things possible and others impossible. But if we change what we think about reality, we can make the impossible possible.

William James thought about reality differently than most of the people of his time, and he passed that thinking on to Gertrude Stein, who helped ignite a revolution in art during the early decades of the twentieth century. There is a delightful story that Stein tells in *The Autobiography of Alice B. Toklas* about William James visiting her in Paris. By that time, the walls of Stein's house were already full of the paintings of soon-to-be-famous artists like Matisse and Picasso. Stein describes the story through the eyes of her companion, Alice:

> Some years after when Gertrude Stein and her brother were just beginning knowing Matisse and Picasso, William James came to Paris and they met. She went to see him at his hotel. He was enormously interested in what she was doing, interested in her writing and in the pictures she told him about. He went with her to her house to see them. He looked and gasped, I told you, he said, I always told you that you should keep your mind open. (*The Autobiography of Alice B. Toklas* 80)

This book is inspired by the exhilarating realization that changing our worldview, and shifting the paradigm we live in, unlocks our hidden creative potentials. Perhaps our greatest historical example of this is the shift in worldview, or paradigm, that brought us from the medieval world to the modern world. The modern world that we more or less live in today was born with a shift into a new paradigm, one that was eventually described as the scientific worldview in a manifesto written by a group of philosophers who were part of a creative circle in Austria known as the Vienna Circle. The worldview they described had been initiated by Descartes and his idea of a universe consisting of three-dimensional space filled with things—with humans as the thinking-things in the universe. This is often referred to as the "Cartesian" worldview and it continues to be the paradigm that shapes our thinking, and therefore, the world we live in today. Undoubtedly, we have been blessed by the many advances in creative potential that came with this enormous shift in worldview. The strides forward in terms of human life that we enjoy in our world compared to the world of Europe in the eleventh or twelfth century are incalculable. We could write volumes upon volumes about how lucky we are to live in the modern world vs. the medieval one. But there are many today that also recognize the potential for another, equally massive, shift in paradigm—a shift that will unleash a new level of creative potentials.

This scientific worldview is largely an extension of ideas that were developed in ancient Greece and rediscovered by scholars of the medieval world. So great is the influence of ancient Greek thinking on our own time that the twentieth-century philosopher, Alfred North Whitehead, claimed that all of European philosophy is merely a succession of "footnotes to Plato" (Whitehead 39). Of all the ancient Greeks, it was Plato—and then Aristotle—from whom we inherited the great legacy that became modernism. The foundations of our things-in-space consciousness, with its separation of mind and matter, has been acting behind the scenes in human consciousness since at least the year 400 BC, when Plato presented his famous allegory of a cave. In *The Republic*, Plato offered a model of reality that set patterns of thinking in human consciousness that continue to shape our minds to this very day.

Plato's allegory takes place in a dark cave where people are sitting in a row facing one of the walls. Behind them is a burning fire, and the light from the fire casts their shadows onto the wall in front of them. They can move their bodies, but they are unable to take their eyes off the wall. The shadows are the only reality these people know. They see their own shadow and think it is who they are (132-133).

If we think about it, even briefly, we see so much in this little scene. The fire is the really real source of wisdom. Really real physical people exist also, but no one has direct access to the really real truth about themselves. The shadows projected on the wall are the only perceived reality they have.

A couple of thousand years later, the German philosopher Immanuel Kant would modernize the language of this view by making a distinction between phenomena and noumena—or reality as we perceive it and reality as it really is (and cannot be perceived). Noumena are the things, in and of themselves, that cannot be perceived directly. The appearance of things, the phenomena, are like the shadows on Plato's cave wall. They are not really real, but they are all the people will ever know.

Mach's and James's radical empiricism offered a radically different way of understanding. It was a view that would later be incorporated into what came to be called "process philosophy." The French philosopher, Henri Bergson, a contemporary and friend of James, was a superstar in Paris and was very busy presenting similar ideas to standing-room-only theaters in Paris at the time when Gertrude Stein lived there. John Dewey was another famous process philosopher, as was Alfred North Whitehead. Gertrude Stein—who we already know worked closely with James and continued to be acquainted with him until the later years of his life—also spent considerable amounts of time with Alfred North Whitehead and his wife in England, and she was a great admirer of Henri Bergson and his philosophy. Undoubtedly, she was also aware of John Dewey through his writings, all of which influenced her attitude towards art and writing.

The worldview that James and Mach were describing was not a collection of solid objects that existed in an expanse of empty space. For them, reality was a succession of experiences that appear one after another. Any sense that we have of three-dimensional space is itself just an experience constructed from the passing show of the stream of consciousness. There is no physical dimensionality in experiences; there may be experiences of physical dimensionality, but those experiences take up no actual space. In his book, Mach mentions a story about someone who wondered how we could fit the idea of a big tree inside our small heads (Mach 27). He uses the story to make the point that ideas don't take up space. The world of pure experience that James and Mach believed in isn't a world of three-dimensional space; it doesn't take up any space at all. It is simply a succession of experiences.

But this is not the way we were trained to think. We have been conditioned to assume that reality is a vast expanse of three-dimensional space filled with things, and we take the same things-in-space metaphor and use it to understand our inner world. We imagine that, inside us, there is an expanse of consciousness—inner space—that holds representations of what we see outside—mental things. If reality is a succession of experiences—or what James would call a "stream of consciousness"—then reality doesn't take up any space. The felt experience of space is a constructed interpretation, not an experience of some actual space. The experience of three-dimensional space that feels so real to us is just a habit of perception, exactly like our understanding of the sun rising in the morning. It may look like the sun is rising, but only because we have been trained to see it that way. Similarly, it may look and feel like we live in three-dimensional space, but only because we have been trained to experience it that way.

The model of reality that we interpret all of our experience through, whether we realize it or not, is a model of physical beings housed in bodies walking around on a planet that floats in a vast three-dimensional expanse of space. Our body comes equipped with five senses that take in information from the world around us and our minds create an inner picture that corresponds to the world outside. We then use our minds to make decisions about how to respond to the world. In order for this model of reality to make sense, we have to imagine that there is someone who experiences the world and then makes decisions to act. We are trained to imagine that we are a thinking-thing in the world or, you could say, an individual achiever. We are the one who not only experiences the world, but understands it, and learns more about it all the time. You end up locked in the experience of a reality that includes an outer material world, an inner world of mind, and a person or ego, that experiences, understands, and acts.

Neither James nor Mach believed that something like an ego actually exists. If we think about the idea of the stream of consciousness, we will likely find ourselves relating to it as a succession of experiences that we have, one after another after another. It would be a bit like watching a movie on the screen of your mind. A movie, or motion picture, is a series of still photos that appear one after another before our eyes in such rapid succession that we don't see individual images, only movement. But if you were to play the film slowly enough, you would see one still photo after another, appearing and disappearing. It is easy for us to think of the stream of consciousness in the same way because it doesn't inherently challenge our worldview. We can still be a person living in a three-dimensional world watching the stream of consciousness pass through our mind. No problem, not so hard to imagine. If we see it this way, we have effectively deradicalized radical empiricism and made it conform to the sensibilities of our things-in-space paradigm. But the alternative is so radical that it is impossible to imagine.

What James and Mach wanted was for us to see ourselves as an occurrence, an affair, of the stream of consciousness, not as a separate thing looking at the stream of consciousness from outside it. To grasp this, you have to embrace the possibility that there is no actual person, physical or mental, that is who you are. There is a constructed sense of being someone, a feeling of being me, and a conviction that I exist. But all of those are experiences in the stream of consciousness, no different than any other experience. There is no inside and no outside, there is no me and no other, there is just experience. Some experiences feel like they are happening inside me, some feel like they are outside, but they are all experiences. There is no self, no entity that hovers beyond the stream of consciousness having the experiences. There is just a stream of experience, and each experience leads to the next one, and then to the next, and the next, and so on.

We do not exist, at least not as the three-dimensional thinking-things that we have been trained to see ourselves as. The feeling of being someone is just another interpretation that arises naturally in the stream of consciousness. We have physical sensations, thoughts, feelings, memories, etc. and we conclude that those experiences are all about us. We assume that someone exists to have all those experiences, but in fact, they are all just experiences, including the assumption that those experiences are about someone that exists to have them. What is so radical about radical empiricism is the fact that everything—including every conclusion about and understanding of ourselves—is just another experience. Reality is a world of pure experience, not an expanse of space filled with things. You could summarize this statement very simply by saying that the only thing that exists is the raw, uninterpreted experience of this moment. Everything else, every notion, idea, and conception we have about what is real, is an imagined interpretation. Those interpretations, through the force of habit, will eventually 'feel' like they exist, but they don't.

We have been trained to think of ourselves as a thinking-thing living in a universe that holds us. But James and Mach want to retrain you to see yourself in a new way. To use James's language, that means: "We live, as it were, upon the front edge of an advancing wave-crest..." (*Writings 1902-1910* 1207). We are the perception that spontaneously arises at the leading edge of the stream of consciousness as it moves ever forward. But remember, we are not a person on that edge; the experience of being a person is one of the perceptions that emerge spontaneously on the leading edge of the stream of consciousness. We are not a person on the edge of the stream, we *are* the edge of the stream. The experience of being a thinking-thing in a three-dimensional world has developed to become a relatively stable habit of perception that reoccurs, over and over again, at the leading edge of the stream of consciousness.

Let's use the familiar experience of reading as an example of how the stream of consciousness moves forward by constantly adding new experiences to itself, experiences that not only add something new but also recontextualize all that came before. You start reading a sentence with the first word, "A." At this point, you don't know much, but you already have a feeling that a specific something is on its way. Now you read the next word, "big." Hmmm, suddenly you can add to the vague sense of comparative size. The third word is "black" and now you have a specific something to picture in mind, something big and the color black. The fourth word is "dog." Finally, you can add a picture to what came before. Now you have a generic image of a dog in your mind, you have a more specific sense of what "big" might mean, and you can see that it has black fur. The word "dog" has added richness to the stream of consciousness. With each new word in the sentence, new dimensions are added to what appears in consciousness.

The entire sentence reads, "A big black dog is about to bite your behind." If we were to give this a little more time, we could go through each word as it appears in the sentence and see how it contributes more dimensionality to the story. When the sentence ends, you have a complete picture that you did not have at the beginning. The meaning of the sentence grew with the addition of each word. The stream of consciousness unfolds like a sentence, growing in richness of meaning with each new experience. The words in the beginning shape and influence the later words, and the later words alter and adjust the way we see the beginning words in retrospect. This is how life unfolds, one experience adding itself to the next as if it were the next word in a sentence. And each new experience that gets added, like each new word in a sentence, adds a host of insight and understanding about all that came before, as well as feelings and insights about what is likely to come next. The experiences of the stream of consciousness keep rushing forth, getting more and more full and rich as they do. There are no people in the stream, only experiences, some of which are experiences of experiencing yourself as a person having experiences.

In order to open your mind up to this utterly alien vision of reality, you have to relax deeply enough that you can start to forget that you exist as a person having experiences. You have to become so utterly at rest that you simply start to see one experience after the next appearing in consciousness. This is what can happen in meditation and why I love to do it. In meditation, you slow down your perceptual mechanisms so much that you see, firsthand, that the only thing that is actually happening is one experience appearing after another. You see that there is no 'you' in there watching it all. The only thing you see are experiences of *feeling like* someone watching it all, and convictions that those feelings are accurate, although, of course, these are just more experiences. If you can relax deeply enough, it will all feel so obvious and so liberating. You will be free of the straitjacket of assumptions of your own existence that have bound you up and stifled your potential for so long. You will see that life keeps moving and growing freely and that you are the movement of life.

This is an aspect of the philosophy that Gertrude Stein was so deeply steeped in while working with William James at Harvard. From the analogy we drew between how sentences unfold and how experience unfolds, you can also see why Stein might have become such a brilliant experimental writer who focused so intensively on words and how they unfold together, affect one another, and create a sense of meaning.

It has been a few days since I wrote the paragraph above. It is 5:34 on a beautiful Sunday morning. I am writing on a round glass table in my kitchen in Philadelphia. On my left are sliding glass doors that look out onto a small enclosed backyard. Although I cannot see it from here, I know that the earth's rotation has only just revealed the sun. In fact, the time mistakenly thought of as sunrise occurred at 5:31 a.m. The light is soft and the birds are loud. It is a good time to write.

Often, when you read a book, you aren't told anything about the author's state while writing it, as if the author's circumstances are irrelevant. But, of course, they are not. I write differently in the morning than I do at night. My consciousness is different in the morning than it is at night. But these factors most certainly affect what I write, even if I don't mention them. A few days ago, I started to get stuck, not knowing where the book wanted to go next. So, I've been reading and waiting for inspiration to return. Slowly, it has become clear that the book wants to move toward a direct discussion about art, something I wasn't expecting.

Gertrude Stein was fascinated by writing. Perhaps it was because of her college experimentation in automatic writing, although she would later distance herself from that work. She came to the conclusion that an activity as complex as writing could not be done completely unconsciously and automatically. She knew that it had taken a great deal of practice to train herself to write automatically, so how automatic was it really? Still, she had been fascinated by the automatic movements that seemed to emerge from what she imagined to be our bottom-nature, and as one of the first modern experimental writers, she never stopped exploring the medium of writing. John Dewey once said that intellectuals think through ideas and representations in their minds, but artists think in the medium of their art. If this is true, then Gertrude Stein thought through her writing. Her art was an exploration of the written word—not only the meaning of the words but the entire process of writing and reading.

After graduating from Radcliffe, where she had studied with William James, Stein—based on James's advice—pursued graduate studies in medicine at Johns Hopkins University. After completing a medical degree, she moved to Paris in 1903 to live with her brother Leo. Over the next few decades, Stein asserted herself in the Parisian avant-garde art scene. She and her Saturday night salons became central fixtures around which a circle of artists, writers, and cultural elites gathered.

Stein and her brother began buying works of art soon after she arrived. They were early patrons of both Henri Matisse and Pablo Picasso. Over time, they gathered a collection of art including numerous pieces that would later become recognized as masterpieces such as Picasso's *Boy Leading a Horse*, *Lady with a Fan*, and *Portrait of Gertrude Stein*. Other significant pieces in their collection included Paul Cézanne's portrait of his wife and Matisse's *Woman with a Hat*. Their paintings hung from floor to ceiling in their small apartment, at 27 rue de Fleurus, where their Saturday night gatherings were held. These salons were alive with conversation and Gertrude Stein offered her thoughts and advice freely to just about everyone.

Initially, Stein's focus was on painters, but over time, she began to attract more writers into her circle. She was, for a time, associated with Sylvia Beach, who ran a famous bookshop called Shakespeare and Co., a gathering place for a group of young writers who would become as famous as the artists featured on Stein's walls—James Joyce, F. Scott Fitzgerald, and Ernest Hemingway but a few. Stein met Hemingway when he was still a young man working as a journalist. She became an important mentor to him for a number of years and influenced his embrace of life as a writer.

It is difficult to judge how much influence Stein had on the art that was developed during the early decades of the twentieth century in Paris, but it is safe to say that it was tremendous. Besides her early patronage of some of the most important artists of the time, she became something of a coach to artists and writers alike. Her views and opinions were sought out by many. And she was almost certainly, directly and indirectly, sharing her understanding of process philosophy with everyone.

However, Stein's writing was so highly experimental, it is largely almost unreadable. Very little of her work, with the notable exception of *The*

Autobiography of Alice B. Toklas, ever found any popular audience at all. But her experiments in writing did impress and influence many of the younger writers that were part of her circles. Still, the question remains: what was she up to? I want to begin to address this question by presenting you with the first three paragraphs of the written portrait that Gertrude Stein did of Picasso:

> One whom some were certainly following was one who was completely charming. One whom some were certainly following was one who was charming. One whom some were following was one who was completely charming. One whom some were following was one who was certainly completely charming.

> Some were certainly following and were certain that the one they were then following was one working and was one bringing out of himself then something. Some were certainly following and were certain that the one they were then following was one bringing out of himself then something that was coming to be a heavy thing, a solid thing and a complete thing.

> One whom some were certainly following was one working and certainly was one bringing something out of himself then and was one who had been all his living had been one having something coming out of him. ("Picasso")

Your initial reading of these paragraphs probably brought on feelings similar to mine when I first read it—annoyance, incredulity ("did she really write like this?"), maybe even dismissal. The famous Harvard behavioral psychologist, B. F. Skinner, who knew of Stein's early laboratory work at Harvard, wrote an article called "Has Gertrude Stein a Secret?" in which he dismissed her work as merely the mindless product of automatic writing. Stein, in turn, dismissed Skinner's accusations saying: "No it is not so automatic as he thinks. If there is anything secret it is the other way too. I think I achieve by xtra consciousness, xcess, but then what is the use of telling him that, he being a psychologist and I having been one" (Mellow 737).

It appears that Stein didn't consider her later experimental writing to be a direct continuation of her earlier experiments in automatic writing. But then what were they? I believe they were, at least in part, her continued thinking—through the medium of writing—about the radical empiricism she had learned from James, and later from Whitehead and Bergson. In an essay called "Composition and Explanation," Stein describes what she was doing with her writing by saying, "There was a groping for using everything and there was a groping for a continuous present..." (*A Stein Reader* 499).

Remember that James's radical empiricism describes all of reality in terms of the relentless growth of the ever-expanding, continuously present, moment. As he describes in his essay "A World of Pure Experience," "The universe continually grows in quantity by new experiences that graft themselves upon the older mass..."(*Writings 1902-1910* 1182). Stein was exploring this idea in writing through the exploration of the meaning of sentences, which she said had no emotion but that grew into paragraphs that could hold emotional content. She was, as she often said, exploring the continuous present.

Another quality of James's view of the present moment is that it contains all past and future moments. Time must be continuous, meaning there can be no break between moments, because if there were breaks between this moment and the last, we would remember nothing—unless we somehow existed beyond the stream of time as some kind of transcendental ego, an idea that James rejected. In addition, there can't really be a past and future that is separate from the present, because everything that is, exists now. There is just a present moment. The experience of the passing of time is an interpretation in the same way that the experience of space is an interpretation. The feeling of time is created because of the way different aspects of the experience of the continually present moment feel in relation to one another. In the always-present moment, there is a focus of awareness which figures most prominently and feels like *now*, but the tail end of all past moments is also present. The moments that feel the furthest in the past are those that have only the slightest bit of tail left, which is why they are so hard to bring to mind clearly. The leading edge of all future moments are also present now, and again, those that are the faintest feel the furthest in the future and are the hardest to imagine.

Stein was groping to find a way to include everything into the present moment of her writing and, subsequently, in her reader's reading. I believe that she was thinking about a world of pure experience and the philosophy of radical empiricism in the way artists think through her medium of writing. I see Stein as a wonderful example of an Artist of Possibility. She expressed some of the most paradigm-shifting ideas of her time in an artistic form that inspired others to achieve creative greatness. Many of the artists and writers who knew her were probably influenced by her radical empiricism, even if they weren't aware of it. If you look at some of Picasso's paintings, especially his abstracts, you will see a world of pure experience being brought to the canvas.

Many of Picasso's most famous paintings depict human faces that appear to be disjointed and disfigured. They can look repulsive because they lack the unity we see in a normal face. radical empiricism would tell us that the unity we see in a face is not there in the stream of consciousness, but rather a construction of our minds. What we see are individual glimpses of the face—first a nose, then an eye, then the movement of hair—as our attention moves and gets caught on separate features in succession. We create the sense of unity. If you look at some of Picasso's more seemingly disjointed paintings—and imagine that he was not trying to represent the face as our habits of perception would eventually unify it, but rather as the collection of immediate impressions from the stream of consciousness—you get a whole new window into what might be happening in his art.

This is a book about art, not the art of painting, or writing, or music, or dance, but the art of possibility. In my opinion, Gertrude Stein was a very successful Artist of Possibility, playing, as she did, such a prominent role in the emergence of modern art that brought the modern mindset along with it. William James was another Artist of Possibility. The most obvious medium of Stein's art was writing while James's was ideas, but I would argue that the deeper artistic medium that they were both working in was possibility itself. They were busy expanding the possibilities of reality by expressing different ways of experiencing and outlining the broad contours of a new paradigm.

CHAPTER 6

The Revolutionary in Art

WHEN I HAD ONLY JUST finished writing the previous chapter, I started to feel the energy of this chapter building to a fever pitch in my body. The energy became so strong that I had to get up from the computer and pace around the room to let it dissipate a little; to be honest, at the moment I'm writing it is still a little too strong for me to type effectively. My hands are vibrating with the energy of anticipation, and my mind is racing with ideas that dart in and out of view. I may need to pace a little longer before continuing because, to be honest, my fingers keep hitting the wrong keys. If I didn't go back and fix things, then the words on this page would lookk something lieke htis.

So I am back at my computer again, a few hours later, after having gone to the park to walk and let the excess energy dissipate. I feel much more able to type now. My mind is working smoothly and my fingers are hitting the right keys.

In the last chapter, I mentioned John Dewey's intriguing notion that intellectual thinkers think using the abstractions of thought while artists think through the medium they create with. This idea was expressed in Dewey's 1934 book *Art As Experience*. I remember being an undergraduate student in physics and noticing that the art majors were carrying that book around with them. The cover pictures a silhouette of a man resting on his side. You view him from behind and there is a bird perched on his hip and another on his head.

Art had been my first love and what I had really wanted to study. I came to the study of physics through a circuitous root. My father always encouraged my art but discouraged pursuing it as a career. "If you love art, become an architect," he suggested. So, for a few months, I practiced architectural rendering from a book. It didn't feel like art to me. My father had always told me that the best job to have was engineering, and after trying my hand at architectural rendering, I decided I might as well study it. It took only one semester to realize that I was not going to get a degree in the subject because I couldn't handle the volume of mathematics I had to learn. Physics was the only class I liked, and I found out you could get a bachelor's degree in physics and avoid at least some of the math requirements. Most importantly, at that time, I was a self-proclaimed atheist and I was sure that physics was the best route to understanding the nature of reality. Still, every time I would see Dewey's book under some art student's arm, I would feel a little pang of longing.

Perhaps that book was simply inserting itself into my mind so that I would find it again, a few years ago, when I was offering a workshop focused on art and artistic expression. Perhaps that workshop was preparation for writing this book. All of the trailing edges of those earlier experiences still exist in this moment, and this moment is being shaped by all of them, and the writing that I am about to do will be shaped by the unfolding of this present moment as it gropes blindly forward from here.

Art as Experience begins with a summary of Dewey's interactionist view of life, the same view that he had already written about, decades before, in his paper on the reflex arc that we've already explored. By 1934, his view was more fully developed and more broadly and simply stated. Dewey saw life as the unfolding of a constant interaction with nature, which included our physical and mental surroundings. Life wants us to remain in harmony; when all of the elements of a local environment are aligned, life moves along smoothly like a boat floating down a river. But circumstances continually shift and knock things out of balance. When things become disunited in nature, an impulse to reunite arises. Energy bursts into the process of life to fuel a reintegration. A process of realignment begins and continues energetically until harmony is once again restored. Those moments when balance and unity have finally been restored, after this exertion of energy, are the most intense experiences of being alive. These are the moments that art attempts to capture and express.

In his book, Dewey shares his understanding of what art actually is. What makes art 'art'? The first thing Dewey wants to make clear is that art is not an object, it is not a painting, or a song, or a dance, or any other thing. Part of the reason Dewey wants to be clear about this is because he embraced the world of pure experience and the radical empiricism that he first encountered in James's *The Principles of Psychology*. In *Art as Experience*, Dewey offers a brief statement of his understanding of radical empiricism: "The past is carried into the present so as to expand and deepen the content of the latter" (24). Experience keeps growing as everything from this current moment spills into the living interaction of now.

Remember, according to James and Mach, no things actually exist; only experiences of things exist. Therefore, art cannot be an object; art has to be an experience. What makes art 'art' is the particular kind of experiential process that it is. And that process has three main components: the artist, the art piece, and the recipient of the piece. Art begins with an inner impulsion in the artist, or the artistic drive. It might begin as a slight nagging, but it grows. It is the feeling that something is missing, that something that needs to be expressed has not been communicated yet. Then, the artist begins their work. They begin painting, writing, or sculpting. Once the artistic process begins, it becomes a communication between the artist and the piece that is being created. As the artist works, the piece takes shape, and then the shape that it takes informs the artist on how to proceed. The artist will be compelled to continue in this way until they recognize that the created work has satisfied the original need that led to the creative impulsion. This interaction between the artist and the work is the process of art. What makes art 'art' is the fact that it was created in this passionate, open-ended, and co-creative way. The essence of art is that the artwork creates itself as much as the artist does, and the artwork shapes the artist as much as the artist shapes the work.

One of the most powerful and productive artistic impulsions was that of American poet Walt Whitman. Whitman worked on his magnum opus collection of poems, *Leaves of Grass*, while living at 99 Ryerson Street in Brooklyn, NY. The impending threat of civil war was creating disharmony, and Whitman was driven to write his book of poems because he believed he could write a poem that was so beautiful that it would allow the nation to avoid the conflict. *Leaves of Grass* was published in 1855, but civil war erupted anyway in April of 1861. The war had not been averted, but Whitman did publish a poem that revolutionized the art of poetry.

His poetry was ridiculed by many in his own time, with the one powerful exception of Ralph Waldo Emerson, who embraced Whitman as the poet that he knew he would become. Today, Whitman is seen as the founder, or at least an early pioneer, of free-verse poetry. That means, generally speaking, that his poems did not rhyme or follow standard rules of meter and line length. He was experimenting with writing in the middle of the nineteenth century in ways that would set the stage for Gertrude Stein's work at the beginning of the twentieth century.

We aren't done with Dewey yet though, because art does not end with the final piece of the creative process between the artist and the artwork. The second half of the process happens when the piece is appreciated. Viewing a painting, reading a book, or listening to a song is not merely a passive activity. As Dewey put it, the "beholder must *create* his own experience" (*Art as Experience* 54). The final appreciation of a work of art occurs when it is engaged with by an audience. That engagement is itself, an active process through which a final appreciation of the art is achieved. In our current paradigm, we are taught to think of perception as a passive observation, not as an act of creation, but Alva Noë, in his 2012 book *Varieties of Presence*, defines perception more actively as "a transaction; a sharing of a situation with what you perceive" (3).

I experienced the truth of this dramatically, many years ago, when I saw one of the paintings in Monet's *Rouen Cathedral* series hanging in the Museum of Fine Arts in Boston. A friend of mine had told me how beautiful one of the paintings was, and so I went looking for it with great anticipation. I found it, and from memory, I believe it had been placed prominently in a corner of a large room. The painting depicted the front of a grand cathedral painted in bright yellows. I stood and looked at the painting.

"Hmmmm, it's OK," I thought. I could sort of see a cathedral in it. It wasn't very distinct, but I could see the steeples and where there were icons sculpted into the walls. I could see the stairs leading up to the big church doors. But, to be honest, it seemed pretty underwhelming to me. I knew that Claude Monet was an impressionist, but even so, it lacked some clarity that seemed necessary to me. Still, my friend had told me it was his favorite painting, so I kept looking at it. I backed ten feet away and kept looking. It was interesting, but nothing really special. In fact, as I looked at it, the bright yellows and whites combined with the blurriness almost felt like it was hurting my eyes. I had to squint to keep looking. Oh my god! I saw it. This was a painting of a cathedral with the bright sun shining on it and into my eyes. It was blurry, not because Monet couldn't have made it distinct, but because, at that time of morning, the brightness of the sun reflecting off of the cathedral and into my eyes would make me squint. For a moment, I felt as if I was transported to a European square in front of the cathedral at daybreak. I felt as if I was seeing it in person. This painting was truly amazing. I was seeing the cathedral exactly as Monet had wanted me to see it. Exactly as he had seen it. The art had been completed...by me!

The point here is to realize that I had to work at this. I didn't just walk up to the painting and see what I was supposed to see. I had to work through whatever preconceptions were blocking me from seeing it. I had to stay with it. I had to relax and change my distance. I had to work at seeing it. I was a participant in the creation of the experience that I ultimately had.

This was Dewey's vision of art as experience. The creation and the beholding of art were two sides of the artistic process: both were important, and together they completed the work of art. A work of art that is never truly seen, is not a work of art yet. I hope, in writing this book, that the awesome power of the process that allows us to co-create reality will be felt by at least some of my readers. When that happens, that reader will feel, in the reading of this book, what I am feeling now as I write it. That is the moment when this book will become a work of art. That is when the book will finally be written.

Having explored Dewey's process-oriented understanding of art, we are now ready to take another look at Gertrude Stein's experimental writing. You can say it is unreadable and cast it aside—and I am sure most people have done that—but not if you are motivated to find out what it is about.

If, like me looking at Monet's painting in the museum, you don't want to look once and give up, then you will surely have to work at reading it. Gertrude Stein's work is demanding. It demands that you engage with it. You cannot just passively allow your eyes to look over the words. You cannot simply read it with ease or leisure. You have to engage. You have to work at it. She makes your own act of reading obvious. She forces you to be active with her in the process of communicating. Her writing is disruptive. It doesn't allow you to just read along and enjoy it. It stops you in your tracks. It challenges all of the habitual ways that you have learned to interpret words. It wakes you up. It forces you into the moment of reading because you have to actively engage to understand.

In doing this, Stein was expressing one of the hallmarks of the modernist avant-garde world of art that she was a part of. The artists and writers in Stein's circles and beyond who identified with the avant-garde movement were not trying to paint beautiful pictures or write entertaining stories. They wanted to disrupt our habitual ways of seeing and understanding. They wanted to make our unconscious habits of perception visible to us. They wanted to make us uncomfortable. The goal wasn't to give us easily recognizable patterns that would allow us to simply look, read, listen, and enjoy. They were giving us art that we had to work with. We had to relearn how to see and understand things in new ways in order to appreciate this art. These artists were breaking the rules not just to be rebellious, but to ignite us to greater conscious awareness. Art was playing a role in the process of awakening.

Perhaps we could say that art of this type is serving a revolutionary function. Maybe there is something akin to Thomas Kuhn's distinction between "normal science" and "revolutionary science" in art too. Perhaps there is 'normal art' that keeps extending the techniques, styles, and ideas already in existence and then there is 'revolutionary art' that challenges the foundational assumptions of the existing paradigm. Revolutionary art would be the art of possibility because it would be aimed at challenging the validity of our current assumptions about what is possible by bringing new possibilities to life.

In this exploration, I do not want to limit the medium of art only to painting, writing, music, acting, and dancing. New possibilities can be brought to life in every human endeavor. For example, the art of possibility can be expressed by a great statesman like Benjamin Franklin. Bill Gates and Steve Jobs certainly created a new world of possibility with personal computing. Scientists like Marie Curie and Albert Einstein changed the way we understand the world. And, of course, social activists like Malcolm X, Martin Luther King Jr., and Jane Addams are powerful examples of Artists of Possibility. In fact, King's short and beautiful "I Have a Dream" speech is one of the most profound examples of the art of possibility—an expression of a future that does not yet exist in a form that inspires and galvanizes the powers of human imagination.

There is no aspect of human life—from the way we take care of our children, to the way we take care of our health, to the way we entertain ourselves, to the way we clothe ourselves—that does not undergo periodic and revolutionary change. And, every time such a leap forward occurs, it is because someone, or some group of people, envisioned a new way of being and stood for it unflinchingly in the face of opposition. These courageous pioneers are the Artists of Possibility who keep our world moving forward.

At the same time that we expand our idea of the arts to include other domains of human endeavor, we should continue to keep in mind these characteristics that make art 'art.' What characterizes art is the interactive and open-ended process out of which it emerges and is ultimately appreciated. The artist feels compelled to express something through a piece of art, and as the piece takes shape through the efforts of the artist, the piece itself informs the artist as to how to proceed in a co-creative process. We could juxtapose this artistic process against a process of construction. If we are building a house, we want the finished house to be as close to the original plan as possible. There certainly can be artistry in the building of a house, but not in ways that result in deviation from the plan. The artistry of building might have to do with how the plans are realized and how the builder contends with unexpected problems, but where the final form of an artistic work is unknown until it is finally birthed, the final form of the house was already clear in the plans.

In light of all this, we will consider the unique role that traditional mediums of art—painting, poetry, writing, music, dance, sculpture, etc.—have played in the awakening and advancement of human culture and consciousness. For our exploration of the evolutionary and revolutionary role of art, we will examine the ideas of one of Gertrude Stein's contemporaries: the Russian artist Wassily Kandinsky. Kandinsky was born eight years before Stein and died two years before her. He moved to Paris in 1906, only three years after Stein had, and did in fact meet Gertrude and Leo at their famous home at 27 rue de Fleurus.

Wassily Kandinsky studied economics and law in Moscow before moving to Germany to take up a career as an artist. From Germany, he moved to Paris and joined the ranks of the radical avant-garde there. Today, Kandinsky is recognized as one of the most important abstract painters of the twentieth century, on par with Picasso and Matisse. In 1911, Kandinsky published a brief, but powerful, treatise on the role that artists play in human development called *Concerning the Spiritual in Art*.

The treatise opens with a harsh critique of "the nightmare of materialism" (2) that "holds the awakening soul still in its grip" (2). In Kandinsky's opinion of his own time, "only a feeble light glimmers in a vast gulf of darkness" (2). Unfortunately, when the human soul encounters this flickering light of alternative possibility, it "trembles in doubt whether the light is not a dream, and the gulf of darkness reality" (2).

During dark times like those he describes, the only thing most people want from art is a little relief. They want art to imitate nature through the use of easily recognizable conventions. Many works of art meet this need and do indeed "feed the spirit" (3). This art performs a critical function. Such works of art at least preserve the soul from coarseness and "key it up, so to speak, to a certain height, as a tuning-key the strings of a musical instrument" (3).

Kandinsky seems to be describing what we have already alluded to as 'normal art.' The function of this type of art is to anchor our senses as closely as possible to the highest possibilities that our existing culture has to offer. Normal art maintains a baseline and holds the human soul to it so that we do not lose any of the ground we've already won. In doing so, it also creates a spiritual buoyancy that tends to lift everyone towards the higher possibilities that currently exist. Presumably, without art playing this all-important and conservative function, the human spirit might spiral downward into ever more crude and self-centered elements of itself. Still, Kandinsky explains, with this function alone "the possibilities of the influence of art are not exerted to their utmost" (3). The true potential of art to creatively bring about a new future cannot be realized with normal art alone.

But there is another function of art, a function that we have previously labeled as 'revolutionary art,' that has a "powerful prophetic strength" (4). All of art is part of the spiritual life of humanity. And the spiritual life of humanity is a movement or development in human experience. It is a movement "forwards and upward" (4). Art, in its revolutionary form, propels humanity's spiritual journey, elevating and expanding the human spirit beyond its current limits. In times of darkness, most people will turn away from artists who express higher possibilities. They cannot see what the artist is pointing toward and cannot believe in it if they do. But the revolutionary artist cannot stop. They are compelled to express what they see is possible, regardless of whether anyone else sees it. Kandinsky, in the opening words of his powerful treatise, is offering a wonderful and evocative description of what an Artist of Possibility is.

He goes on to offer a model of the development of the human spirit. He first likens our collective inner development to a triangle with its peak pointed upward. In that narrowest section there are very few people, and often, at the very tip, only one. These are the visionaries who see things that are possible, yet remain invisible to the rest of humanity. "Even those who are nearest to [the visionary soul] in sympathy do not understand him" (6). The history of human spiritual progress, Kandinsky tells us, involves leaps forward that are inevitably impeded by new obstacles that prevent further growth. "But there never fails to come to the rescue, some human being, like ourselves in everything except that he has in him a secret power of vision" (4).

There are artistic visionaries at the topmost peak of the human triangle, but Kandinsky maintains that artists exist at every level of humanity. Throughout the entire triangle, along each horizontal line, there are artists who see beyond the limits of their current level and—in so much as their art is breaking through to the next level up—they are playing a revolutionary function. Each artist is compelled to strive upward, and many of those around them hunger for the spiritual food that their art can provide. The artist hears a voice that is inaudible to most and "almost unknowingly...follows the call" (9). That call is felt as a mysterious and "super-sensuous" stirring of the soul (15). During times of cultural darkness, when the higher possibilities of spirit have been reduced to only a thin and flickering light in the distance, art is the place where the new future will first reveal itself to those who have the eyes to see it. "Literature, music and art are the first and most sensitive spheres in which this spiritual revolution makes itself felt" (14).

CHAPTER 7

Genius and the Evolution of
Consciousness

THE APPEARANCE OF WASSILY KANDINSKY at the end of the last chapter has charted a course clear through to the end of this book, which has spoken and offered its own vision of where it wants to go. Because of this, I have had to let go of several of my darling ideas in order to remain faithful to the artistry of writing, but I move forward undaunted. The next moment of inspiration will always come to the rescue, and one after another, these moments of heightened clarity that illuminate the way forward like lightning flashes in a dark sky will unerringly carry this book to its as-yet-unknown final destination.

We start with John Dewey's view of life as an affair of affairs; a multi-dimensional self-orchestrating system of interaction. Life manifests on many levels; there is the physical world and all of the energies through which physical objects affect one another, there are the dynamics of living nervous systems that are constantly anticipating and responding to their physical environments, and there is the conscious realm of emotions and thoughts and identities. All of these layers dance in a constant flow of give and take that constitutes the movement of life. And, if left unimpeded, the flow of life hums along, requiring only the minimum level of conscious awareness. The intelligence that is expressed in harmonious, a merely unselfconscious perception that moves according to what instinct and reactivity dictate.

Our human experience of this effortless flow of life occurs each and every day when we complete mundane tasks without being aware that we are doing them. We take a shower and get dressed without conscious memory of what we have done. Certainly, consciousness was required from us along the way, but only at the most basic level. For the most part, life simply lived itself through the habits of our routine. Under normal harmonious conditions, the patterns of stepping over the edge of the tub, toweling ourselves dry, inserting one leg at a time into our pants, etc., are never impeded, and so, no demand is ever made requiring us to become fully present and aware of what we are doing. And when it is time to leave the house, we don't remember any of the details of what we just did.

We can, if we want, call this minimally conscious movement of life "normal life." There is an energy and intelligence in normal life, but it is minimal. Life prefers it this way. Life loves to economize and not waste energy unnecessarily. If there is no reason to stir up higher levels of consciousness, then those levels will be allowed to remain dormant and inactive. Only when there is a demand due to a blockage in the flow of normal life does an additional burst of energy erupt into the system. When the natural, normal flow of life is impeded, energetic excitement bursts forth to stimulate action and awaken consciousness.

We experience this excitement as focus and intensity. When, in the midst of our morning routine, we realize that we don't have a single pair of clean socks to wear, suddenly, our habit of choosing a pair of socks and putting one on after the other is interrupted. The normal energy of life has nowhere to go. We suddenly become present and awake. Of course, it is our custom to look at this exclusively from our human vantage point, but we can also see that it is not us, but life, that has a problem. Maintaining a harmonious flow is life's purpose, and when that flow gets blocked, life calls for an awakening of consciousness to restore it. Some interruptions of flow require the specific consciousness of human beings, and when such interruptions occur, life calls on us—stirring us to a higher level of engagement. Once the problem has been solved, and the natural and normal flow of life has been restored, the demand for consciousness is relaxed and normal life returns to its more economical and less actively conscious flow.

Human beings can be awakened to many different levels of consciousness. Waking up to find a pair of socks certainly requires a level of conscious awareness, but probably only just beyond the relative unconsciousness of normal life. The subtle stirrings that call artists to create are a much higher frequency of energy. These deep stirrings are not aimed at disruptions in the merely physical level of being, but occur at spiritual levels of being. When spiritual harmony is disrupted, the artist is called upon to restore the free flow of spirit. That is the higher role of normal art; it plays a conservative function in the sense that it maintains the harmony of normal spiritual life.

The model of life that we are working with offers a clear distinction between normal art and revolutionary art. Normal art maintains the free flow of spiritual life, by which we mean the flow of subtle levels of consciousness. Normal art holds our inner attention on those values, attitudes, perceptions, and understandings that represent the highest possibilities that our culture has yet to attain. When the flow of these higher possibilities becomes blocked, art in its normal function restores the harmony that has been disrupted.

Revolutionary art is called upon, not to restore the harmony that has been lost, but to instigate disharmony when a need for further growth appears. In order to spur the emergence of even higher possibilities in consciousness, art, in its revolutionary function, disrupts the existing harmony. There are times when the limits of human consciousness are too tight to allow for the flow of life to proceed harmoniously. Like a plant that has outgrown its pot, consciousness needs to be uprooted and replanted somewhere with more space. Consciousness periodically needs to expand because its ceiling has become the inhibitor of life's flow. Life needs new possibilities to flow through it so it awakens the Artist of Possibility to elevate and expand consciousness in new ways. The stirrings that enliven the souls of revolutionary artists are faint glimmers of as-yet-unrealized potentials. They see these potentials and feel compelled to manifest them. The job of revolutionary art is twofold: first, it must disrupt existing habits of perception and being and then create opportunities for new ways of perceiving and being to emerge and stabilize.

Human art forms, with art having the widest possible definition, serve an evolutionary function in the process of life. The stirrings of the Artist of Possibility are inspiration from a future that is possible. Life, it seems, doesn't just want to maintain balance and harmony, it also grows. And the process of higher growth begins within subtle inner domains that can be influenced and affected by the creative expression of art. This is a model for the evolution of consciousness that combines Dewey's process view with Kandinsky's understanding of the spiritual nature of art.

In his 1917 essay "Art as Technique," the Russian literary critic and theorist, Viktor Shklovsky, wrote about what we are calling the revolutionary function of art. He saw clearly how petrified human habits of perception cut us off from actual perception. Once habits have solidified, we no longer perceive the actuality of things, we simply experience our habits. We live in a world cut off and isolated. The isolation and separation generated through the solidification of perceptual habits blocks the road to further growth and disrupts the possibility of further flow. In this constrained state, Shklovsky says: "We do not see [things] in their entirety but rather recognize them by their main characteristics. We see the object as though it were enveloped in a sack. We know what it is by its configuration, but we see only its silhouette" (Shklovsky 4). Life's preference for economical flow leads us to stop looking at things once we think we already know what they are, like recognizing something covered with a sack.

Imagine a rocking chair covered by a blanket. You see the draped blanket and you can tell that underneath is a rocking chair, but you cannot actually see the chair. You have no idea what color it is and no idea what it is made out of. In fact, you can't ultimately be certain if it is, indeed, a rocking chair. You could always pull up the blanket and discover that what you thought was a rocking chair was something else entirely. Our habits of perception, at their best, facilitate the economic flow of life with the least possible mental expense; at their worst, they hide the truth of reality from us by covering the actuality of existence with a blanket of ideas, concepts, and assumptions.

The buildup of perceptual habits dulls our experience of life, "and art exists so that one may recover the sensation of life; it exists to make one feel things..." (Shklovsky 5). Art, in short, wakes up our dulled senses and brings them back to life. It re-energizes and sharpens our perception of things.

"The technique of art," Shklovsky writes, "is to make objects 'unfamiliar,' to make forms difficult, to increase the difficulty and length of perception because the process of perception is an aesthetic end in itself and must be prolonged." And a few paragraphs later he adds, "Art removes objects from the automatism of perception..." (Shklovsky 5).

Shklovsky's view of art seems to me to be a perfect description of what Gertrude Stein was doing with her experiemenal writing. The following passage from Shklovsky's essay could easily be a description of Stein's writing:

ponder

> ...the artistic trademark is that in the artwork—that is, we find material obviously created to remove the automatism of perception; the author's purpose is to create the vision which results from the deautomatized perception. A work is created 'artistically' so that its perception is impeded and the greatest possible effect is produced through the slowness of perception... Poetic language must appear strange and wonderful; and, in fact, it is often called foreign...(Shklovsky 11)

I want to remind you that although models can be useful ways of helping us think, we should not confuse them with pictures of the really real underneath. Mach, as we said, believed scientists should not try to ascribe any underlying meaning about reality to their models. That didn't mean not making models, and it didn't mean not making up descriptions about what the models represented; part of the usefulness of a model is the way it creates an image of what might be happening. Mach maintained that we never forget that we don't know what is going on underneath our models. There is very little chance—in fact, probably almost none—that our models have described reality accurately. It is hard to even imagine that language could hold the ultimate vision of reality, even if we knew what it was.

Scientists use metaphysics when they believe that their explanations about reality are true. We want to stay metaphysically open, ontologically agnostic, and use our models to help us think—and ultimately to live— without getting pinned down to them.

But what does "helping us think" mean, you ask? It means supporting the

119

full realization of the communication at hand. It means supporting you as the reader to see what I, the writer, see. My words on this page are an attempt to convey to you something that I am passionate about. I am not passionate about a model. I do not think the model that I am sharing is the truth about reality. I am using the model as a tool to influence your perception so you see what I see. The famous "finger pointing at the moon" metaphor is particularly useful, where seeing the moon is the goal while the pointing finger is the means. If we get too caught up in looking at the finger, we will never see the moon. Or, if we want to update this metaphor, we can imagine a telescope pointing up into the night sky. The series of lenses and mirrors of the telescope affect our sight as it passes through them, allowing us to see things that we could never see without it. But if we spend all of our time walking around the telescope looking at it, we will miss all that heavenly glory. Mental models are not objects to look at, they are instruments to look *through*.

As an undergraduate, I did my senior research working with an astronomer who had a thirty-inch diameter telescope in his garage. That means the lens was thirty inches wide and that the telescope itself was about twenty feet long. I remember that I had to learn to see through the telescope. I would put my eye up to the eyepiece, but until I got used to it, my eye would focus on the glass of the lens rather than on the stars beyond. I had to learn to relax my habits of perception and allow my eyes to look through the lens and not at it. As you relax and allow your focus to wander into the lens, you start seeing the stars behind it. With practice, your eyes will automatically look through the glass to the stars. This is what we want to do with mental models.

Art itself can be seen as the creation of models to communicate feelings. Leo Tolstoy, in a book called *What is Art?*, describes the essence of art as the state of mind of the artist infecting the perceiver. Art occurs when the spectator, reader, or listener actually feels what the artist is feeling. In this shared experience, the perceiver experiences the joy of union with the artist and with any others who similarly appreciate the art. According to Tolstoy, art unifies people with a common inner vision. "Art," he declares, "...is a means of communication, and therefore also of progress—that is, of mankind's movement forward toward perfection" (Tolstoy 123). Art is created in service of the evolution of feelings, from the more coarse and self-centered to the more subtle, expansive, and compassionate. Art for Tolstoy, as for Kandinsky, serves our spiritual growth.

The goal of normal life is conservative because it wants to flow along as inexpensively as possible. The normal flow of life prefers to be as habitual and unconscious as it can be, because, in that way it conserves energy. As long as life can flow along unimpeded, it will simply lie back like someone resting in a boat floating down a smoothly flowing river. But, in turbulent times, when the river rushes and froths, we must wake up, grab our oars, and consciously and strenuously navigate the rapids. These are the times that are the most exciting, when we feel most alive. Overcoming adversity in life is what wakes us up to an acute sense of conscious awareness—demanding that we bring forth our best and most conscious efforts to get through the challenge and restore harmony.

Imagine normal life as a river flowing from left to right. The goal of normal life is to flow. It calls us into conscious action only when it needs us to help with a disturbance—we get aroused to presence to find our lost car keys, we step in with clarity and receptivity to mediate a dispute between co-workers, we devise a solution to the problem we face in building a house, etc. Life wakes us up and calls us into action when she needs us, and we are roused to conscious action to serve her. We are one of the many means she has at her disposal to maintain the flow of normal life.

The river is a model depicting normal life, but there is also a spiritual life. Spiritual life moves along a different line of axis, into dimensions beyond what we can see. It doesn't move from here to there, it moves from what is to what can be. It is a movement into possibilities that do not exist yet. It is important to realize that the current of normal life has its own evolution and is constantly manifesting new things. But what I call the upward drift of spiritual evolution is a growth in the range of what is possible. Normal life fills out the things that spiritual life makes possible.

The river of life that we have been describing as "normal," has a depth to it. Along the bottom, the water is brown and filled with sediment, while at the surface, the water is clearer and allows more of the light from above to shine through. The entire three-dimensional world that we call our universe is that river and all of its depth. But that river flows through a wider expanse of dimensionality than we are able to perceive directly. Our current habits of perception only allow us to discern the river from the surface to its bottom. We believe that what we see is all there is. What we are normally unaware of is that the river of our universe is gradually expanding upward into new dimensions of being.

Spiritual life, or spiritual evolution, moves from the bottom of the river to the top, and then, beyond the top. Called by the glimmering light that she sees above the current surface of reality, the Artist of Possibility reaches energetically upward to meet that light and create works of art that can reflect that light into the river below. As Kandinsky said, there are artists throughout the entire depth of the river, and each of them is captivated by the brightness they see above. The combined reaching of all of these artists generates an upward drift in the river itself, a buoyancy that lifts people from the deeper regions gradually upward toward the top and, ultimately, beyond. But this current does more than lift things toward the surface, it also creates a momentum in life itself that allows the entire river to rise up into the higher dimensions above.

Art is always concerned with the spiritual dimension of life and the spiritual evolution of our universe. That means that it is primarily focused on the upward expansion of possibility and not the normal flow of life from left to right. The impulses that invigorate the artist to create are, in some way or another, directed toward whatever glimmer of light from above the soul of the artist has access to. The inner vision of the artist is captivated by the light of possibility and irrepressibly drawn towards it. The normal work of art, which is in itself extraordinary, is to depict and communicate the highest realms of possibility that can be imagined. Throughout the depths of the river of life, there are artists who point our gaze upward to the clearer waters above. The normal mode of art reflects back to everyone (with the eyes to see) the most beautiful, honest, and good that currently exists. The highest forms of love are expressed in normal art and displayed to inspire and uplift everyone. Artists are the engine of spiritual growth.

In using the word 'artist' here, however, we expand its definition to include much more than painters, writers, and musicians. The entrepreneur who creates a business that is itself an expression of higher possibilities is an artist. The spiritual teacher who articulates principles that uplift the gaze of the inner eye is an artist. The restaurateur who creates a beautiful environment that awakens the imaginative powers of all who eat there is an artist. And yes, of course, the painter, the writer, and the musician who connect to the highest potentials of the human soul are also artists.

The most revolutionary art occurs along the top edge of possibility. Beyond this edge, further movement is blocked because the current habits of perception cannot open wide enough to embrace what is above. The calcified, habitual ways of seeing and being cannot go any higher, and as long as we remain encrusted in them, we remain stuck. The revolutionary artist, or perhaps I should say, the artist in her revolutionary mode, must find a way to liberate our awareness from habitual patterns of perception. By confronting us with images and ideas that cannot be easily absorbed by our minds in their current configuration, the revolutionary artist creates a sense of discordance and, in so doing, manufactures a disruption in the flow of life. Life, in turn, responds by unleashing the energy of consciousness in an effort to restore harmony. The revolutionary artist instigates this emergence of higher consciousness with her art. She does more than point to the clearest waters currently in existence, she actually lifts the surface of the river into previously unrealized higher potentials.

Reading this over again in future, I feel compelled to mention one of the drawbacks of the model that I have presented. Namely, it makes evolution seem like a linear progression. But evolution, as I have come to understand it, is not a linear progression; it is an expansion of possibility. It means there is more and more that becomes possible as we progress. But that expansion does not happen smoothly along a straight line. It appears to be a messy affair. It lurches forward, gaining new capacities and, at the same time, losing some that it had. Sometimes expanding what is possible involves reconstituting possibilities that have been lost to us. Evolution is growth, and growth does not necessarily happen along a neat path. That being said, we can continue now and see how our model can help us understand the universal function of genius and the role it plays in the evolution of consciousness.

123

The rush of conscious awareness that life unleashes when her harmony has been disrupted emerges in human beings as bursts of genius. These are the moments when we see clearly what has, until now, been hidden from view. When the veil of ideas, concepts, and assumptions has been lifted from our eyes, we see again, as if for the first time. This clear-sightedness frees our minds from the slumber of automated modes of perception and habitual patterns of thought. Our awareness is free to see freshly and our minds can think with originality. We are liberated into a consciousness capable of finding novel solutions to transcend the disruption.

Genius was a lifelong preoccupation of Gertrude Stein's. She wanted to cultivate the genius in others, surround herself with geniuses, and, in fact, considered herself to be a genius. In *Psychology: Briefer Course,* William James wrote, "Genius, in truth, means little more than the faculty of perceiving in an unhabitual way" (*Writings 1878-1899* 309). Genius for James, and Stein, involved the heightened sensitivity that comes when our awareness has been liberated from the habits of familiarity. In her book *Lectures in America*, Stein characterizes genius by describing its essence as the feeling of "being most intensely alive" and explains that this occurs when we are both "talking and listening" at the same time (170). She goes on to clarify that we are "talking and listening....not as if they were one thing, and not as if they were two things..." (170). To help explain this, she adds a metaphor: "like the motor going inside and the car moving, they are part of the same thing" (170).

I have already mentioned that my life has been dedicated to spiritual pursuits. My artistry of possibility has been to explore, articulate, and teach spiritual practices and mystical philosophies. Earlier, I spoke about what I call the first and second surrenders of spiritual practice. The first being the purely passive letting go of everything, and the second the more active, but still oddly totally passive, letting go into the subtle stirrings of a higher being that begins to move us. When Gertrude Stein describes genius as a state where you are both "talking and listening," I hear a wonderful description of what I have felt and called second surrender, this more active/passive state of surrender that I also like to refer to as "creative illumination."

You see, I discovered something magical during my many years of devoted meditation practice. I was taught that meditation was a purely passive practice of total disengagement with whatever arises in consciousness. Hour after hour, I would sit in meditation and just allow everything to be exactly the way it was, without engaging in any way at all. I was learning how to give up all effort to manipulate or control any aspect of my experience. It was a practice of inner freedom and divine indifference, and through it, I discovered the free-floating consciousness that is the essence of our being.

I also discovered something else. In the free-floating space of deep meditation, I would experience subtle spiritual energies that would bubble up to the surface of awareness. These energies would move me emotionally. I would feel allured by them. They seemed to be inviting me somewhere and I felt compelled to follow them. But in the context of my practice, I would simply leave them alone. Many hours of meditation were spent in this state of deep spiritual longing and divine temptation.

After over a decade of very focused and intense practice, something unexpected happened. One day, in the middle of a meditation retreat, I was so overcome by the desire for awakening that I took what felt like a huge risk: I didn't just let it go. I wouldn't say that I actively engaged with it either, though. I just let myself be carried away by it. I relaxed the effort to remain still and allowed the wave of spiritual energy and inspiration that had arisen in my practice to take me. This peculiar effort of allowing myself to be carried away is what I am reminded of when I hear Gertrude Stein mention talking and listening at the same time.

The retreat that I was attending at that time was the most significantly transformative event of my spiritual life, and it was there that I would later have my first Kundalini experience. I chronicled my journey through that miraculous time in a short book called *The Miracle of Meditation*, and I can say in all honesty that everything I share in this book was revealed to me during that retreat, and has been reinforced, expanded on, and refined, over and over again, many times since.

I remember, as if it were yesterday, the moment on that retreat when I experienced creative illumination for the first time. It was only the second morning of what would turn out to be two months on retreat, and the twelve of us were meditating outside. I was sitting cross-legged with my arms resting on my thighs. I had only just begun when I felt a pleasant energetic tingle in my right arm. It felt like my arm was falling asleep, except it didn't feel quite like that either; it was too soon for my arm to be falling asleep. It all happened so fast. At the moment when the tingle arose, I just decided, or perhaps was guided, to let it overtake me. I relaxed and allowed it to spread. Soon the sensation had engulfed my whole body. I was sitting in a cloud of mildly ecstatic energy. It was so peaceful and so blissful that I knew I could sit there forever.

That choice to relax and be taken is difficult to describe. It feels like it happens somewhere exactly between being active and passive, like talking and listening at the same time. That is what I believe is the space of between-ness that I learned about from the spiritual teacher Richard Rose. The space of between-ness is active and passive at the same time. It is both a place of highly energetic intention and complete surrender to whatever happens. It is a space of magic where all of our creative energy is available to be directed by powers beyond us. I believe that this is the state of genius that Gertrude Stein was referring to. I believe that all of the Artists of Possibility that we explore in this book discovered that space and created their art from it. I also believe it is that space out of which creative illumination occurs. It is the state where we are completely and energetically engaged, and absolutely free and available.

That moment in my practice opened me up to a completely new dimension of spiritual work. I first explored this amazing possibility in meditation, but over time I have found that the actively surrendered state of creative illumination is where I write from and even, at times, live from. It is a space of genius because, in that state, we are moved by currents of wisdom beyond what we normally have access to. By liberating our awareness from its habitual patterns, we inevitably begin to experience subtle energies inviting us into deeper illumination. Once these energies begin to arise, we are no longer served best by remaining completely passive. In these moments of revelation, of genius, we are invited into a journey of discovery. Creative illumination means allowing the energies of our deepest insights and revelations to overtake us and carry us into realms beyond imagination.

I never met Richard Rose myself, but I did have a friend who had been part of a small community of students who lived with him. My friend had lived in that community for over fifteen years and the stories he told me about that time of his life intrigued me. I have to admit that I found something wonderful and bizarre in what Rose taught; his teachings have a certain pessimistic slant that doesn't totally appeal to me, yet I find it captivating nonetheless. His conception of between-ness captured my imagination the most. As I understand it, Rose explained that all energy arises in the space between two or more things, the space of between-ness. Electrical and magnetic energy occurs between positive and negative poles. The energy of friction happens between two solid surfaces that touch. The energy of the mind happens in the encounter of awareness with ideas and feelings.

Rose also asked us to look at the parasitic relationship that all living things have as part of a chain of sustenance. One form of life becomes nutrition for another, sometimes without having any idea that it is providing energy for some higher form of being that is completely invisible to it. Rose points out that we, as human beings, expend much more energy than we need to live. Our big brains, with their massive energy consumption, seem dramatically over-suited to the purposes of acquiring food and shelter. It is well known that our brains consume more energy, by far, than any other organ of the human body. In fact, brains use a full twenty percent of the entire energy produced in the body (Swaminathan). It is a very expensive machine to maintain.

Richard Rose wondered what exactly all that extra energy is being used for. His conclusion was that there must be a higher form of being that we are feeding with all of our extra psychic energy. We are not the highest form of being in existence, and we are producing more energy than we need because that energy is serving the needs of beings vaster than we can perceive. Rose did not speculate about what form of being we might be serving. It might simply be that our psychic capacities have been granted to us in service of life itself. As we have talked about, when life is in need of our genius, she activates it in us. Or, who knows, perhaps there are other life forms that need our energy to survive; perhaps we play a

127

critical function in a universe beyond our imagination.

There is something interesting to ponder here. Spiritual and artistic pursuits have occupied human beings for our entire history. But why? Sometimes it is said that spiritual pursuits have consumed so much human attention because of our need to find security in the immense mystery of life that we are thrust into. Art is similarly seen as providing the consoling power of beauty in the midst of the often harsh realities of the world. These conclusions are certainly reasonable, but isn't it also possible that our spiritual and artistic passions are in service of some higher form of life?

Of course, I am not offering up this speculation in any attempt to determine what is really real, but merely to open up the possibility that we exist somewhere in between realms of being that are incomprehensible to us. Perhaps we are not the crowning achievement of existence, but a small part of a reality much bigger than we can understand.

I leave this chapter with a quote from William James, this time from his book *A Pluralistic Universe*: "The drift of evidence we have seems to me to sweep us very strongly toward the belief in some form of superhuman life with which we may, unknown to ourselves, be co-conscious. We may be in the universe as dogs and cats are in our libraries, seeing the books and hearing the conversation, but having no inkling of the meaning of it all" (*Writing 1902-1910* 770-771).

In the remaining chapters of this book, we will be visited by a number of Artists of Possibility who were convinced that they were communicating with higher forms of being; sometimes divine, sometimes a higher part of ourselves, and sometimes alien. It is my belief that opening ourselves up to our full creative potential involves embracing the possibility that there are higher forms of life—however we want to imagine them—that can express themselves through us. And the place where we can open up to these higher beings—or perhaps to the higher aspects of our true Self— is in that mysterious space of between-ness, the space exactly between supreme intentionality and utter disinterest. It is uncannily the same as the space within which you feel like you are talking and listening at the same time, giving and receiving both at once.

Yes, these ideas can get weird, and we will explore a couple of pretty strange versions of it before we are done, but bringing new possibilities to life is a strange occupation. Everything that has ever been truly new looked bizarre when it first appeared. Almost every revolutionary artist was misunderstood, dismissed, and ridiculed in their own time. They might have preferred it otherwise, but in the end, they didn't create art for recognition, but because they were called to.

CHAPTER 8

Angels of Imagination

IN FEBRUARY, MARCH, AND APRIL of 1871, Ralph Waldo Emerson traveled twice each week from his home in Concord to Cambridge, Massachusetts, to deliver a series of lectures at Harvard called *The Natural History of the Intellect*. They would be the last public lectures he would ever give.

The Natural History of the Intellect was a fitting theme for Emerson's last public talks because developing such a history had been one of the primary ambitions of his life, first mentioning the notion in his journals in 1837. In this final set of lectures, Emerson illuminated on what we could call his theory of conscious evolution.

During one of the lectures, "Genius," Emerson said, "The eye of genius looks through to the causal thought. Whilst the world of men give undivided heed to fact, Genius has been startled by perceiving the fact to be a mask, and detecting eyes that peer through it to meet its own" (*Natural History* 72).

What do these two sentences mean? What is Emerson trying to say? There is so much meaning that we can pull out of this small piece of text. The first is that genius is a living being. It has eyes and it sees. But the vision of genius is deep; it looks beyond the surface of things to the inner thoughts that caused those things to come into existence in the first place. The world around us, the arena of our daily lives, is a world made up of facts—not inner causal thoughts, but conceptual ideas that label everything around us. Genius is startled. It wakes up. It springs to life with the realization that the facts of the world are just a superficial covering. Beneath that covering, the eye of genius sees another pair of eyes looking back. Every seemingly solid thing is a covering, shielding from view a living being that possesses an intelligence of its own. We thought we were the only living things amidst a world full of lifeless facts, but in the startling awakening of genius, we see that we are actually part of a living universe, and with the right vision, every element of that universe is revealed to emanate from the same living source.

"Genius," Emerson tells us, "is a delicate sensibility to the laws of the world, adding the power to express them again in some new form" (*Natural History* 69).

"[It] is a reception from the Pure Intellect—a ray from that on the world in which we live." Genius is an awakening to what Emerson describes elsewhere as the "Soul of the World" (Cooke 315). Genius "unsettles everything" and demonstrates "absolute confidence in the Eternal Prompter" (*Natural History* 72-73).

Emerson is speaking in a language that I think both John Dewey and Gertrude Stein understood, but Emerson makes a more direct appeal to the higher intelligence that is personified as a being with eyes that see. We are, somehow, normally unable to see the living intelligence that exists just behind everything we can visually observe. We seem to have lost our capacity to directly perceive the soul of the world. But that deeper vision wakes up in us, at least from time to time, when the living reality of the world shows itself and shines through some fact in front of us. We thought we were just looking at an object and suddenly we see the higher being behind it.

The idea of the soul of the world is mentioned in another lecture from this series called "Imagination." Everything in the world, "seas, mountains, timber, metals, diamonds and fossils," is unknown to us until we see the real spiritual truth that is hidden behind the surface. The "Soul of the World," or the "Eternal Prompter," pours itself through everything and compels some of us to use whatever means we can to express and reveal that "one fact of Being." This singular living intelligence that we are is also looking back at us through the ordinary world that we see. That "one fact of Being" looks through our eyes out at the world, and in our beginning moments of genius, sees itself looking back (*Natural History* 34).

This ultimate Being wants to be expressed in the world. Emerson describes how "the true poet rushes to deliver his thought, and the words and images fly to him to express it." He is both expressing (talking) and receiving (listening). Genius is a spontaneous act of co-creation. The poet writes and the words flow to her from the "Soul of the World." The source of the poem, or the art, is the confluence of the two working in concert. The purpose of imagination, and presumably of genius, Emerson claims "is to domesticate us in another nature." Our higher wisdom wants us to abide in a different reality (*Natural History* 39).

Moments of genius are moments when we see through the veil of the familiar and glimpse the living reality beneath it. Creative acts that emerge from genius are emanations from a higher Self. True art emerges from the most profound imaginative source. It occurs only when we are able to see directly into the true source of being, and then surrender ourselves to a process that allows that source to express itself.

This brief discussion of two of Emerson's lectures is an act of hermeneutics. Hermeneutics is the deciphering of the meaning of a text. It is the art and science of textual interpretation. The word was originally a reference only to the interpretation of Biblical texts, but what Emerson is laying out for us in these two essays is hermeneutics with an aim to decipher the meaning behind the natural world. Nature becomes something similar to a text that can be read, and our expression of the meaning that is revealed to us calls into being a reality that had once been hidden.

The spiritual hermeneutics of Emerson parallel the work of the twentieth-century French scholar of Islamic mysticism, Henry Corbin. I first heard of Henry Corbin in Gary Lachman's brilliant book *Lost Knowledge of the Imagination*. In this book, Henry Corbin is credited with coining the phrase "the imaginal realm." This was a term that I was aware of but had never known the origin of. I see this beautifully evocative term as pointing to the same magical space of between-ness where the work of creative illumination takes place.

Early on in his career, Corbin was very interested in the German philosopher Martin Heidegger. Heidegger's philosophy was hermeneutical. He did not believe that reality was a collection of objective facts that we could know just by observing them. The reality of the world was inherently meaningful, and the truth had to be discovered through a process of disclosure. We had to interpret it. This idea captured Corbin's imagination and he became the first person to translate Heidegger's work into French. In fact, it was through Corbin's translations that Jean-Paul Sartre and Maurice Merleau-Ponty first read Heidegger, which helped spark the expansion of the philosophy of existentialism.

Spiritual hermeneutics would become a central part of Corbin's understanding of mystical Islam and adds a rich and wonderful dimension to our understanding of between-ness and creative illumination. After learning about Corbin from Lachman, I discovered that Corbin's work has been deeply explored in books written by Tom Cheetham. One of those books, *All the World an Icon*, offers a dramatic and wonderful vision of a world of angelic beings and the co-creative disclosure of those beings.

While Richard Rose explained that energy arises in the juncture between things, Corbin describes the imaginal realm as a realm of being that exists between the unknowable ultimate reality of pure unity and the solid world of three-dimensional objects here on earth. Corbin was a scholar of mystical Islam and a theologian, and so I think it's safe to say that the imaginal realm is a realm of being that exists between the mystery of God and life on earth. This magical in-between realm is a space of spiritual creativity, or what Corbin called "active imagination."

One of the many things that I find so fascinating about Corbin is the reality that he had been acclimated into—or as Emerson would say— domesticated into. That reality is a totally personal one, which means that it is entirely made up of a hierarchy of beings. At the top of the hierarchy is something we could call God—the ultimate source of meaning and truth. Below that, there are worlds upon worlds of angelic beings, followed by the world of physical manifestation that we know so well. Everything here on earth, every person, every object, every thought, *everything*, corresponds to some angelic being. Each of us, in fact, has a spiritual other half in the form of an angel. We are a projection of that angelic being upon the earth and, through a process of spiritual hermeneutics that is called "ta'wil" in Islamic mysticism, we can reunite with our angelic self by becoming a perfect reflection of it in our life.

Human beings have lost touch with the angelic realms. We now live within a dichotomy that separates God from earth. We have become disconnected from our source. The severing of man from God occurred as a result of the Age of Reason and the shift to a worldview that is rooted in a belief in objective reality. We stopped seeing the universe as alive and began to see it as a collection of facts. Corbin saw the beginning of this shift occur when St. Thomas Aquinas embraced Aristotle's philosophy over Plato's.

The subtle realms occupied by the angels have become inaccessible to us in a world dominated by objectivity. The universe of things in three-dimensional space, in which truth is seen as fixed and visible, cannot accommodate the angelic realms. We have lost access to those realms of being, and unfortunately, that means that we have lost access to the very realm that is essential to our spiritual development. By cutting ourselves off from the subtle realms of the angels, we not only created an unbridgeable divide between us and God, but we also lost all connection with the means for inner growth.

The mystical vision of Islam is vast and sweeping in scope, and I cannot pretend to understand the depth of that cosmology from the reading I have done. But what I want to share with you is the deeply resonant understanding of reality that was transmitted to me when I read *All the World an Icon*. Initially, as I read descriptions of Corbin's angelic realms of being, I found myself visualizing literal angelic beings with glowing bodies of light and wings. I was involuntarily combining the three-dimensional things-in-space model of reality with images from my Catholic upbringing to generate my picture of the angelic realms. But, when I let go of that framework, something wonderful appeared.

After letting go of my Cartesian/Catholic angelic interpretation, I simply saw a realm of being, a world, but not a three-dimensional world. Instead, the angelic world was a world of pure experience, just like we have discussed, but that was superimposed on and coexisting with, the familiar world of pure experience. Everything around me suddenly held two realms of being. One was held in the visible surface facts, the other was the angelic world—equally present, but beyond my ability to interact with. Once I stopped imposing the idea of space and form, the angelic realm felt as if it was right here, right now, but invisible. It isn't located any distance away because there is no space to worlds of pure experience. The angelic realms are not located somewhere else; they are here.

According to Corbin, each of us has an angelic half. Our angelic half is not a being with form; it is the idea that initiated, and now fuels, our material existence. It is the angelic essence of who we are. The path to God is initiated when we make direct contact with our angelic essence—our angel guide, if you will, or our higher Self. In that moment, we come in contact with the deepest and most authentic aspect of our individual self. By aligning with that essence and allowing it to be expressed through us in life, we move into the angelic realms and unify with our essence. At the very same time, the angel's being also grows and becomes fuller. The angelic part of us becomes more complete because we are manifesting more of it. Two dimensions of being—the angelic and the material—merge and ultimately become one. The process of unifying with our angelic half is our path to wholeness and authenticity. Cheetham likens this to the Atman of Hindu philosophy. Brahman is God, the one Self behind all of life, and Atman is the highest form of our individual self. Ultimately, Brahman and Atman are one and I am That! When we realize our authentic being the divide is dispelled and we become one with God.

Corbin's angelology is beautifully poetic and evocative of the magical and otherworldly quality of the imaginal world, which is the meeting place between our human self and our angelic self. Spiritual growth and fulfillment occur in the interaction between the human realms and the angelic realms, or perhaps we could say, borrowing again from the Hindu tradition, between the subtle realms and the gross realms. This in-between space, which we lost in our embrace of a worldview rooted in objective facts, is the space of creative illumination, or what Corbin calls active imagination. In that space, we discover a new reality, but it is not a reality that exists independently of us, or that is just waiting for us to find it. It is a reality that is constructed as we creatively imagine it into being. This is the imaginal realm. Working in the imaginal realm is another way to understand what this book is about. The imaginal realm is the realm of genius, and Emerson describes the co-creative artistry that occurs there by noting that "the true poet rushes to deliver his thought, and the words and images fly to him to express it..." (Natural History 37).

The word hermeneutics is derived from Hermes, the winged Greek messenger god who brought messages from the divine realms to the mortal realms. But Hermes didn't just carry messages; he interpreted messages from gods to humans. So too, then, is hermeneutics the act of interpreting messages from God. This work of interpretation is called ta'wil and is done in the imaginal realm. Corbin explains the essence of ta'wil as "a matter of harmonic perception, of hearing an identical sound... on several levels simultaneously" (qtd. in Cheetham 87).

In order to engage in the imaginal realm, we must develop the ability to perceive in multiple dimensions at once. We must embrace the reality of a pluralistic universe—a universe where more than one thing is true at the same time. That is why the paradigm of objective fact has no access to the imaginal realm. The framework of immutable facts cannot accept multiple realities; it cannot expand to embrace paradox. It is stuck in a single view of reality and a new view can only be embraced as real by making the old one false.

The imaginal realm is not a place that exists somewhere else. It is simply the deeper dimensionality of what is. We don't find the imaginal realm by looking somewhere else, but rather by changing how we look at what is already here. When we embraced a world of objective fact, we forgot that everything that is here in front of us is a symbol for a deeper truth. We must look beyond the surface of reality, learn to read the symbols, and allow them to carry our vision deeper, as if on winged feet, to a divine realm of perception. We must de-literalize what we see and look through the surface into a new layer of meaningfulness.

As I read about Corbin's vision of reality, it was clear to me that he was saying we cannot think of the imaginal realm as symbolic in a simplistic way. The things around us aren't just labels for something else; they're portals. They don't tell you something, they transport you to it. What we discover when we look deeper, is that imagination is not just a way of inventing things in our heads; active imagination is an organ of

[handwritten: title². Mark-making as co-creating]

perception. It is a co-creative effort that generates what it perceives while it perceives it. Sounds a lot like talking and listening at the same time, doesn't it?

Our life is a hermeneutical project. It is a reading of the unique way that divinity, the soul of the world, manifests to us. The divine does not show up in the same way for everyone; each of us is given a unique glimpse of the higher realms. Our spiritual work is hearing, interpreting, and expressing how God has revealed him or herself to us. We write the story of God's vision to us. We express our unique glimpse of the heavenly realms. Through the process of ta'wil, our life becomes a living exegesis, or a written explanation of a sacred text. We continually express our developing understanding of the divine message as it is revealed to us.

I am so happy to be able to have had the chance to share my experience of Henry Corbin with you here. Gertrude Stein, William James, Richard Rose, Henry Corbin, Anaïs Nin, Ramakrishna, and Philip K. Dick, to name a few, are all Artists of Possibility who have inspired me in different ways. And, looked at through the lens of Henry Corbin's beliefs, they were all linked by the fact that they were engaged in hermeneutical life projects by constantly examining and interpreting their experiences of life. They were each compelled to express the unique vision of possibility that was given to them to share. Their lives demonstrate the intensity of focus and commitment of someone who knows that their ultimate fulfillment can only be found in the sharing of their inner vision.

 [handwritten: my book]

If you are reading this book—and you must be—I believe it is because you also have been given a vision of a possibility. You must also know that your ultimate fulfillment is linked to sharing it. You may have already begun, or you may not know how to start, but you know that you have been shown a possibility that is yours to share. This book was written to inspire you and support you in that pursuit.

I relate very personally to the words of Emerson and Corbin in their discussions of between-ness and creative illumination because of the way these ideas have manifested in my own life. Only eight days after my Kundalini experience on the meditation retreat, something else happened.

Our last meditation on each day of the retreat was between nine and ten at night. On this particular night, I was struggling with sleep. I felt very tired, but I was determined to stay awake. I was making tremendous effort to stay alert and attentive. My body ached with tiredness. I had a headache and the quality of my awareness was murky. My nervous system felt overstimulated, as if an electrical current was running through my veins. It was very unpleasant, but I was determined to remain awake. I held my body rigidly stiff, I meditated with my eyes open, and I maintained an inner sense of tension, all in an effort to ensure that I didn't fall asleep. After sitting like this for some time, a thought passed through my mind. The voice said, "You are not really tired." But it didn't feel like me; it felt like someone else's voice in my head.

I have to admit that I did occasionally hear voices like this during meditation—thoughts that were worded as statements made to me, but not by me, generally with a ring of unquestionable authority. At the time of this retreat, I had never heard of Henry Corbin, but now I see that this experience could be interpreted as guidance from my angelic half. At the time, I thought that it certainly couldn't have come from me, because I knew for a fact that I was tired.

Do you see how that works? Knowing something as a fact excludes all other possibilities. William James called this kind of knowing "vicious intellectualism" (*Writings 1902-1910* 677). Ordinarily, we rest so immovably secure in what we think we know that we are not available for the appearance of any other alternative. In that rigidly fixed state of mind, there is no access to the angelic realms—or any other possibility—because we are already adhered to a single reality as if it is the only possibility there is. This is how facts kill the active imagination.

So, getting back to the story, I heard this voice in my head saying, "You are not really tired." And in that instant, I realized that it was true; I wasn't tired at all. I was completely awake and alert, looking through an exhausted body. Suddenly, I was not my body. I was the conscious awareness passing through the body. The body was tired, even the mind was tired, but that which was aware of the tired mind and body was just as clear and awake as it ever was, and I was That! I felt completely liberated. I was not tired at all. I was free. I was having the experience

141

of exhaustion, without being identified as if it was me. I was simply a free-floating awareness that was shining through a tired body. The me that had been looking at the *fact* of a tired body had looked so deeply that it had discovered that something was looking back, and that something was me.

I didn't make that experience happen. I don't even know how it happened. An incongruous statement appeared in my head and I believed it. I had been guided, as if by an angel, to look in a different way. I was having two experiences at the same time. They both existed simultaneously and completely overlapped each other. They both included the exact same sensory data, but interpreted it in two completely different ways. The normal experience of being exhausted was still there, but now the very same physical sensation of exhaustion was also seen from the vantage point of a liberated awareness that was wide awake. I was overtaken by a sense of euphoria as I looked at every detail of exhaustion from this freer position. It was amazing. The mind and body were just as exhausted as they had been only a minute before, but now *I* was wide awake. From this vantage point, the details of the tired mind and body were fascinating and, as I scanned over them, I was flooded with insights and realizations. Not only was I not tired anymore, even while sitting in a body that was in desperate need of sleep, but I realized that I had *never* been tired. I had always been this free-floating awareness shining through the experience of a body.

When the bell rang to end the meditation, I slowly stood up and walked to the building where my room was. Nothing changed. My body arose off the cushion and started walking. I was walking with it, but it didn't feel like I was moving. It felt more like watching a movie. I felt stationary, watching through the eyes of a body that was moving. I was still meditating. I got home and laid down to sleep. As I lay there, I felt my entire body go totally numb. I knew that my body had fallen asleep, but I was still awake. Then I saw my mind slowly shut down. The experience of my body laying on the bed faded until it was gone. I was aware of nothing. It felt like, or I interpreted it as, being a free-floating awareness in the blackness of space.

Eventually, a scene emerged, and I was in it. I was at a gas station being pulled to pieces by a group of strong men. They were chanting "you've got to go," over and over again. I felt the pain of my limbs being torn apart, and I saw the men all around me. It was all so real—for a moment—before I realized that I was dreaming. My mind had turned back on, as if someone had flipped a switch, and it had created the whole scene. I could experience it through the interpretation that I was the person being torn apart while simultaneously experiencing the whole scene as a free-floating awareness. I didn't have the language to describe it in this way at the time, but now I see that I was being introduced to the strange, miraculous, and mysterious possibilities of spiritual hermeneutics. The raw sensory data was the same in either case, but I had the power to interpret it differently. I could change my interpretation of what was happening, and that changed everything about it. My interpretation of the experience determined which world I lived in—the one where I was being torn apart at a gas station, or the free-floating spiritual awareness witnessing the human experience of dreaming. The choice seemed to be mine.

The dream ended as abruptly as it had begun. The mind simply shut down again without any warning, right in the middle of the scene. I was once again floating in the blackness of nothing. The insights and realizations continued to flood through me. I had never been anything other than this awareness. Every night before this, I was lost in the belief that I was sleeping because I was experiencing a body that was sleeping, but I was always awake. This free-floating awareness was always there, resting behind every experience I had ever had, even my experiences of deep, unconscious sleep. Even when I was not aware of it, it was aware—and I was That. I realized, without a doubt, that when my body ceased to function and I died, I would simply rest in the peace of nonexistence. I would continue to be a free-floating awareness, only then I would not have a body to identify with.

It was crystal clear that this same liberated awareness is what I was before my body was born. This worldly physical existence was like a dream to that otherworldly awareness. The body appeared as if out of nowhere at birth, and just as abruptly, would disappear at the moment of death. Awareness was there before birth and would remain after death.

In the morning, I felt my body wake up. The numbness ended and the vital energy once again ran through my limbs. My eyes opened and I stood up, but nothing changed. I had been there, aware, before my body woke up, and I was there and aware now. The awareness didn't feel like it had woken up; it had already been awake. Awareness didn't feel like it had moved; it was simply seeing through a body that was moving. I floated through breakfast, then in and out of the morning meditation sessions and lunch, all the way until the end of the day. Nothing changed at all. My body and mind kept shifting from one experience to the next, but the awareness was just aware. I went through another night of conscious sleep. It wasn't until the third morning that I realized I had, at some point that night, lost consciousness and fallen asleep the old-fashioned way. I woke up that morning as if I had been gone all night. I felt some disappointment that the awareness had left me, but mainly I was overwhelmed with gratitude at all that I had seen. I continued the retreat with renewed dedication and much more ease.

In this experience, you can see how sensation—raw experiential facts—were constantly accompanied by interpretation. Our sensation of life is turned into experiences by our interpretation of it; we create the story of our life as we go. Corbin and Emerson saw that most people were stuck in a single interpretive framework, a single paradigm, that is, the paradigm of being an isolated being in a three-dimensional universe full of material things. It is the paradigm of an objective reality that appears to us as immutable facts. That paradigm does not allow for alternative interpretation. Only one thing can be true at a time, and so, in order to move into a new interpretive framework, we must prove the old framework wrong. One of the aspects of the current paradigm that can never be questioned is the insistence that only one thing can be true at a time. That is the viciousness that James was pointing to.

Creative illumination means the willingness to step into a different reality, which means the willingness to embrace and create a new interpretation out of the sensuous experience of life. I was playing a creative role in interpreting a reality in which I realized a deeper reality of ever-present, free-floating awareness. But that was not the only possible interpretation of the 'facts.' I could have interpreted what was happening as a story about having insomnia, or about starting to go insane. There are many possible stories that can be embraced to shape the reality of raw sensation. And different interpretations will manifest different experiences of reality. And the place where this kind of reinterpretation of reality is possible is the imaginal realm. You can't just do it in the solid world; that would be fantasizing. This was different. I was interpreting a new reality, but the reality that I was interpreting was also real. Experiences like this have led me to see meditation as an act of resting in the imaginal realm. It involves becoming comfortable in a state of availability, ready to be moved into a different interpretation of reality—if your angel arrives to show you one.

Both Emerson and Corbin were opposed to fundamentalisms of any form. They saw reality not as a fixed thing but a fluid one. In spiritual work, when we have an experience of a different reality, the fact-based habits of the current paradigm will tempt us to interpret any new possibility as the really real possibility. We may move from one fixed reality to another, but in either case, we remain rigidly adhered to one interpretation, one world, one form of reality. We still have no access to the imaginal realms where reinterpretation is always possible. In his writing, Emerson advocates that we maintain a "soft bond between poetry and reality" (*Natural History* 70). "For the state of being," he says, "... is always divinely new,—ever flowing from its ineffable fountain" (*Natural History* 73). Security in this liberated way of being does not come from the certainty that we know the truth. It comes from "absolute confidence in the Eternal prompter" (*Natural History* 72) that guides us from one world to another as we realize the full potential of our True Self. We must live in a state of readiness to be moved because "Genius," Emerson tells us, "unsettles everything" (*Natural History* 72).

Recently, someone asked me how I reconcile the experience of a Kundalini awakening with the experience of constant consciousness. I don't. I feel no need to reconcile those two experiences and make them fit into the same world. I live in a plurality of worlds. Right here, in this experience of being, many possible worlds can emerge out of various possible interpretations. More than one thing can be true at a time. Whether you see these as worlds, as the German philosopher Martin Heidegger did, or as beings, as Henry Corbin did, the end result is the same. We don't live in just one world. We don't have to fit every experience into a single narrative. More than one thing can be happening at once. Like William James, I am more comfortable with this pluriverse than I am with any singular universe. As Walt Whitman said, "I am large, I contain multitudes" (Whitman 43).

Meditation, as resting in the imaginal realm, means resting in a state of availability, ready to be moved into a different interpretation of reality if your angel arrives to show you one. This understanding of meditation is well suited to the task of creative illumination and active imagination, but to some, it would seem to stand in contrast to the spiritual lineage that I was trained in. During the twenty years that I spent living in a spiritual community, I worked in the lineage of Ramana Maharshi. Ramana is known as one of the greatest saints of twentieth-century India, and is revered the world over for his simple and pure teachings of Advaita Vedanta.

Ramana taught the very simple practice of Self-inquiry that essentially consists of asking yourself, "Who am I" in the face of every experience you have. What you discover by doing this practice is that you are always the awareness that is aware. Once you discover that, you simply rest your attention there forever. Your spiritual work is done, because you've found the truth of who you are. Some might interpret my experience of constant consciousness as the discovery of the true Self, and I believe that it was. In that case, some would wonder why I don't just rest in that truth and forget about all these stories of angels, Kundalini, and interpretive frameworks.

On the one hand, I could say—in all honesty—that I haven't moved from that experience of pure awareness; how could I? I have never lost faith in the fact that that liberated free-floating awareness is the deepest source of my being. I don't doubt that I am That. I don't experience any fear of death because I know who I was before I was born and who I will be after I die. So, in a sense, I have not abandoned the experience I was blessed with. At the same time, I feel no compulsion to assume that it is the only reality that exists. In fact, I feel compelled to continue to open myself up to more of reality's possibilities. Why? You might ask. Why be open to more when you have found the deepest source of Self? I don't know why. It is not a rational choice. It is just what I feel compelled to do. In a sense, I have no choice, and in that way, I am perfectly aligned with the teachings of Ramana Maharshi.

Ramana's teaching was of total surrender to the true Self based on the realization of non-duality—which means the recognition that nothing and no possibility could exist outside of that Self. "The Self itself is the world; the Self itself is 'I'; the Self itself is God; all is Shiva, the Self," he said (Maharshi 11). In this recognition of radical inclusivity, there is no need to do anything to make things other than they are, because everything and its opposite is part of the Self. The practice is simply to surrender and stop making any effort to change anything. In fact, according to Ramana, we are powerless to change anything: "What is destined to happen will happen. If you are destined not to work, work cannot be had even if you hunt for it; if you are destined to work, you will not be able to avoid it... So leave it to the Higher Power..." (57-58). In another passage, Ramana describes the surrender of one's life with a metaphor:

> Whatever burdens are thrown on God, He bears them. Since the supreme power of God makes all things move, why should we, without submitting ourselves to it, constantly worry ourselves with thoughts as to what should be done and how, and what should not be done and how not? We know that the train carries all loads, so after getting on it why should we carry our small luggage on our head to our discomfort, instead of putting it down in the train and feeling at ease? (12)

I believe that the life of an Artist of Possibility is a surrendered life. If it had been my destiny to meditate for the rest of my life in a monastery—as I had hoped for at one time—it would have happened. But it didn't happen. It was my destiny to teach, and to write, and to offer this very book to you. Our angel guides, the Self, or the energy of genius, illuminates the way forward. We do not choose the path, we follow it. Of course, at the same time, it is a path of our own making. We are building the path that we follow. We are reading the words as we write them. We are talking and listening at the same time.

I have been quoting from *The Spiritual Teachings of Ramana Maharshi*, a small and extraordinarily powerful book of spiritual wisdom. It has been

147

about three years since I last read it carefully, and it is interesting for me to see how different the experience of reading it again now is from it was then. Right now, I am bringing to the reading a head full of the writings of Gertrude Stein, William James, Ralph Waldo Emerson, and Henry Corbin. The philosophy of radical empiricism and ideas about imagination and genius are influencing my reading. Reading is not a passive activity; when we engage with a book, we create an understanding. The understanding that emerges from the reading is created through the interaction between the content of the book and us. Everything that we are, and everything that we are bringing to the reading, shapes the resulting understanding. The act of reading is hermeneutic in nature. The same book is a different book to every reader, and it is a different book to the same reader every time she reads it.

What I see in my current reading of Ramana is how his instructions for meditation sound, to me, like instructions for resting in the imaginal realm. When asked to define meditation, Ramana says, "It is abiding as one's Self without swerving in any way from one's real nature and without feeling that one is meditating" (34).

The part of this instruction that strikes me most right now is the final instruction to meditate "without feeling that one is meditating." Ramana is asking us to do the practice but to forget ourselves doing it. We let go of our identity as someone meditating and allow the practice to continue. We let go of our memory of ourselves and forget the fact of our existence. When asked how long one should practice, Ramana answers: "Until the mind attains effortlessly its natural state of freedom from concept..." (35). He associates meditation with the act of dwelling in non-conceptual awareness, calling it "...the state of being free from all mental concepts" (35). This seems an idea parallel with the process of de-literalizing that liberates us from the world of rigid facts.

In meditation, as we let go of our conceptual grasp on the world, we enter a dream-like state of fluid and free consciousness. It can sometimes feel as if we are falling asleep, and yet it doesn't really feel like we are sleeping, either. When a disciple asks Ramana about this sleep-like state, wondering if he is failing in his practice, Ramana replies, "'Like sleep,' that is right. It is the natural state" (78). Ramana would refer to meditation—the practice of abiding in the Self—as our true nature, or our natural state, which is free from thought. This dreamy state of free consciousness reminds us of the liminal state between waking and sleeping that is today called hypnagogic. In Ramana's teachings, there is a similar idea to our natural state: the experience of resting in the Self.

We can also see, of course, the essence of between-ness in this state of consciousness. The paradoxical nature of which is even more obvious in passages such as:

> Although the Self is real, as it comprises everything, it does not give room for questions involving duality about its reality or unreality. Therefore it is said to be different from the real and the unreal. Similarly, even though it is conscious, since there is nothing for it to know or to make itself known to, it is said to be different from the sentient and the insentient. (44)

The Self is neither real, nor unreal; it does not perceive, but it is also not unconscious. It is a very strange kind of between-ness that Ramana invites us into.

I feel no conflict between my background in Advaita Vedanta and my current explorations of creative illumination and genius. As a pluralist, I feel no need for the two to reconcile with each other. At the same time, I am amazed at how much of what I am now so fascinated by—in terms of the liminal state of between-ness—can be found in the spiritual tradition that I spent so much time in.

Now, there will undoubtedly be some people familiar with the teachings of Ramana Maharshi who will feel that I have misunderstood those teachings or misrepresented them. They will think that I've got Ramana all wrong. But, I would say that relating to Ramana as if he were a fact that you are either right or wrong about is counter to everything we are exploring. I am not trying to discern the truth about Ramana; I am encountering him freshly now. A person is not just an objective fact that you are either right or wrong about. A person is an encounter. During the years that I lived in a community and was dedicated to the path of Advaita Vedanta, I encountered Ramana one way. Three years ago, as I prepared to give a meditation training, I encountered Ramana a different way. And today, as I am writing a book about the inherent mutually creative nature of life, I encounter yet a different Ramana. Encountering a person is something like reading a book; we encounter them differently each time.

The pluralism that William James taught frees us from needing to relate to the world, or to other people, as objective facts of experience. Is there a Ramana that exists independently of the way he is experienced? Does anything exist independently of the way it is experienced? Is there an objective world that exists beyond any experience of it? And if so, how could we possibly have any idea that it exists at all? I present Ramana to you because his teaching has been so important to my life, and because I truly believe he is one of the brightest spiritual lights of the modern age. I also present him to demonstrate how reality doesn't just exist but is co-created in our encounter with it. This happens at the more mundane levels of the world, and as Corbin shared with us, it happens in a very profound way in the mystery of the imaginal realm.

CHAPTER 9

A Passionate Surrender of
Life to Art

I WANT TO REITERATE THAT, when discussing Artists of Possibility, we are using the word "artist" in its widest possible sense. I feel the need to keep saying this because I notice that in this book, and indeed in the very chapter you are about to read, I often refer to writers, philosophers, painters, or mystics. These are the forms of art that my life has been devoted to and it is natural that they come up in my writing.

As this book has unfolded, I have had the privilege of introducing you to some of the Artists of Possibility that I find inspiring and who have helped me tell the story of this amazing form of art. These individuals are all very different, but if you look from a far enough distance, you will find some common characteristics, and perhaps chief among them is that of passionate dedication.

Artists of Possibility are deeply passionate about something, a possibility that doesn't yet exist, but that they can see in the dim distance of a future not yet realized. They are captivated by a vision, and their lives become a total expression of the pursuit of that vision. They cannot help themselves. They press on. They don't necessarily move in a straight line; they zigzag this way and that. They follow the trail wherever it leads. The expression of their vision is the thing that matters most; all other aspects of life are secondary. In the end, their life expresses what moves them, and it is hard to know if their life created their art, or their art created their life.

These artists are all different, and they are not necessarily perfect, in fact, they're often far from it. William James suffered from depression and deep insecurity his entire life, teetering at least once on the edge of taking his own life. Gertrude Stein could be egotistical and competitive with her associates. John Dewey, on the other hand, seems to have been a fairly upstanding and morally clear individual. And of course, Ramana Maharshi, who walked away from his childhood to live the rest of his life as a revered sage at the base of a mountain, seems by all accounts to have been a true living saint. The personal characteristics of these individuals vary dramatically from one to the next, but the passionate dedication they had to the unique possibility of their inner visions reveals a unifying characteristic.

There are certain Artists of Possibility who captivated the imagination of my youth and have served as inspirations during my entire life. One of these was the twentieth-century writer Anaïs Nin, who was born in France to Cuban parents. At the age of eleven, after her father had left the family to be with a younger woman, Anaïs moved with her mother and new stepfather to America. On the ship, Nin wrote a letter to her father, describing coming to America in glowing terms in the hopes of luring him home. She never mailed the letter, but writing it initiated a practice of keeping diaries that she did continuously until her death at age seventy-three.

Nin moved back to Paris in 1930 with her first husband Hugo and became part of the literary avant-garde. Nin was in the generation after Gertrude Stein, but it appears that she did meet her at 27 rue de Fleurus. However, Nin was not particularly impressed with Stein or her circle of writers. In an interview only two years before her death, Nin said, "The younger writers thought that they were passé, too 1920's. We were trying to be our own writers, and we didn't have much respect for Hemingway or Fitzgerald. We weren't thinking about them so much as about ourselves. I went to Gertrude Stein's place once and found her very tyrannical" (Bailey).

My relationship with Anaïs Nin began when I was in my twenties. I had read some of her fiction and parts of her diaries. I don't remember how I first found out about her, but I was intrigued from the start. She has always felt like an old friend that I would come to see infrequently throughout the rest of my life. Her writing was intimate and personal. She wanted to record, as accurately as possible, her spontaneous first impressions of life. She was fascinated by what she could learn about herself through an unmitigated, unfiltered, and immediate examination of her emotional reactions to everything. Anaïs Nin's life was a demonstration of her ferocious commitment to being authentic and unconventional, and, given that she was a young woman living in the 1930s, her outrageous life is even more astounding. It was not a perfect life, but it was a life deeply, fully, and exhaustively lived.

In her diaries she writes, "I don't really want to become normal, average, standard. I want merely to gain in strength, in the courage to live out my life more fully, enjoy more, experience more. I want to develop even more original and more unconventional traits" (*Diary of Anaïs Nin* 112) And elsewhere:

> To hell, to hell with balance! I break glasses; I want to *burn*, even if I break myself. I want to live only for ecstasy. Nothing else affects me. Small doses, moderate loves, all *demi-teintes*—all these leave me cold. I like extravagance, heat...sexuality which bursts the thermometer! I'm neurotic, perverted, destructive, fiery, dangerous—lava, inflammable, unrestrained. (*Incest* 152)

In Paris, she met Henry Miller. At the time, she had already been published, and Henry was young and looking for his first break into writing. It was Anaïs, and her first husband Hugo, who funded the printing of Miller's masterwork *Tropic of Cancer*. The book was initially banned from publication in the United States, but nonetheless established Miller as a literary giant of the twentieth century. Nin fell in love with Miller's wife June and had a long and passionate affair with Henry as well. When her first diary was published in 1966, her relationship with Miller was a central piece of it, but her marriage to Hugo was omitted entirely. The reason for such an obvious omission? By that time, although Anaïs was still married to Hugo and lived with him part-time in New York, she was also married to a second man she lived with part-time in California. She didn't want her two husbands to find out about each other, so she left Hugo out of the book, telling him that she wanted to spare him the publicity.

There is something profoundly courageous about Anaïs Nin's

commitment to being so utterly unconventional. In her freedom, she challenges the conventional parts of all of us. I like to think of myself as fairly unconventional, and yet Nin challenges me to question the possibility that I am more conventional than I might like to think.

She was passionate about writing and was almost desperate to be recognized for her craft. She felt certain that her writing was important and wrote constantly throughout her life. She lived with a wild, and at times, almost reckless, abandon. No one could tie her down, although many tried. She wanted freedom, spontaneity, and unconventionality, and desired to express them all in writing that was wild and free and raw. She wrote in the immediate wake of life, directly from the first reactions in a stream of consciousness.

Nin wrote two articles on the craft of writing. In one, "Realism and Reality," she speaks about the immediacy of emotion that she tries to capture in her writing, describing it as an attempt to express the unconscious mind. To her, this direct expression of the unconscious was the new writing that needed to replace the old form of plot, character, etc. The old form had little to offer now, because we had discovered the unconscious: "the conventionalities of the novel can no longer communicate what we know...the new novel will be one in which everything is produced only as it is discovered by the emotions: by associations and by repetitions..." (*Portable Anaïs Nin* 235).

I can hear Stein's "talking and listening," ideas in this quote, even if Nin had found her unimpressive. In fact, although Nin may not have thought much of Gertrude Stein, there is a great deal of Stein's literary sensibilities in her. Both Nin and Stein were influenced by psychology, Stein through her academic training with William James, and Nin through her years of psychotherapy with Otto Rank—one of Sigmund Freud's closest colleagues. In her writing, Nin was exploring the ideas of the unconscious that came from Sigmund Freud, which is both similar to and different from how Stein tried to capture the continuous present.

Nin felt strongly that our discovery of the unconscious mind had changed everything, and that the structure of the novel had to change with it. Since we had come to know how much more there was going on beneath the surface, superficial plots and storylines were no longer adequate or interesting. In order to express the new world of the unconscious, we needed a way of writing that could express more than what we were conscious of. Our writing would have to be so free and spontaneous that it carried messages that even the author was not aware of, an idea that Philip K. Dick later explored.

Nin did not want to give up all realism in writing. She understood that "While we refuse to organize the confusions *within* us we will never have an objective understanding of what is happening *outside*" (239). Writing doesn't need to abandon all realism, but it does need to do more than merely report about events. In "Realism and Reality," Nin goes on to say, "Reportage, the other extreme from unconscious writing, is not reality either, because facts stated objectively, scientifically, statistically without the artist's power to communicate their meaning do not give us an emotional experience. And nothing that we do not discover emotionally will have the power to alter our vision" (237).

save
usyc
art!

Nin describes herself as a poet writing in prose. "I intend," she said, "the greater part of my writing to be received directly through the senses as one receives painting and music" (233). Her books, she claims, "take place in the unconscious" (233). But she asserts that her writing is different from poetry because it contains "both the symbol and the interpretation of the symbol" (233). Once again, we see a possible connection to talking and listening at the same time. Nin captures the richness of the unconscious in symbolic form while also interpreting those symbols and sharing those interpretations with her readers.

In her second essay on writing, "On Writing," Nin describes how what she is advocating for "requires a fusion of two extremes, which have been handled separately, on the one side by the poets, and on the other side by the so-called realists" (241). This fusion of two extremes reminds me of what Richard Rose said: that all energy came in the space between things. Nin seems to have tapped into a potent source of energy, and in her diary writing, she claims to have discovered certain elements that make the new writing possible. First, and most importantly, she insists the writing must be natural and spontaneous. Secondly, it must deal with "..the immediate present, the warm, the near, being written at white heat..." (*Portable Anaïs*

Nin 240). Writing with intensity and immediacy in this way allows the author to develop "a love for the living moment" (240). Finally, she makes a statement about the necessity of having a "personal relationship to all things" (240), which sounds like the idea of a radical empiricist.

In a particularly telling passage, Nin seems to reveal the reason why she pursued a life of intense interpersonal relationships, complication, and drama.

> Like the modern physicist the novelist of today should face the fact that this new psychological reality can be explored and dealt with only under the conditions of tremendously high atmospheric pressures, temperatures and speed, as well as in terms of new time-space dimensions for which the old containers represented by the traditional forms and conventions of the novel are completely inadequate and inappropriate. (239)

Anaïs Nin's life is an invitation to the possibility of a wild and intensely creative freedom. By resting your attention on your immediate, emotional reaction to the experience of the living moment, and then expressing that living moment as faithfully as you can, you inevitably pull up symbols from the unconscious that you can then interpret on the spot. I see such a strong correlation to William James's experiments with nitrous oxide. Nin was essentially doing what James was doing but without the chemical. The immediate emotional response that comes directly out of the living moment has not yet been structured by the mind. It is still in its original, untainted form, like James's first thoughts coming back from a nitrous oxide blackout. And, just like James, Nin wanted to record those thoughts directly from the unconscious abyss onto paper. At the same time, she also wanted to shape them with interpretations that would make them intelligible and decipherable to the reader.

Nin's invitation was more than just a new way of writing. It was an invitation to self-actualization. In those first unsullied responses to life, you find your true Self—the person that you are before you tell yourself stories about who you are. In those moments of raw, unguarded reality, where you're not controlling yourself and you emerge truly spontaneously, you reveal yourself to yourself. Attaining self-actualization was the obsession of Nin's life. She wanted to be the fullest expression of herself that she could be. She didn't want to limit herself in any way, and her passionate pursuit of radical authenticity and self-actualization, despite the messiness it so often created, inspired millions of people to live a more uncompromising life for generations.

Another Artist of Possibility that has felt like a friend to me my whole life is the modernist Portuguese poet Fernando Pessoa. I first learned about Pessoa in high school when I was learning the Portuguese language, and my Portuguese teacher—who had studied at the famous University of Coimbra in Portugal—introduced us to his poetry. In some ways, his reclusive and quiet life of tedium was the polar opposite of Nin's wild and fiery life, but he was just as equally dedicated to his writing and wrote constantly during his entire lifetime. In fact, the quality that most connects them is their total dedication and commitment to a life of the imagination. Nin's diaries sometimes read like fiction, making you wonder if she were self-consciously orchestrating chaos in her life to create scenes to fill the pages of her diaries. Pessoa, on the other hand, lived the rather nondescript life of a dedicated but struggling writer, whose real life was experienced in and through his writing more than it was in the world around him.

Pessoa was born in Portugal in 1888. His father died when he was five years old. Two years later, he traveled with his mother and stepfather to South Africa, where he lived for the next ten years. At the age of seventeen, he moved back to Lisbon where he would live out the rest of his life, virtually never leaving the city again. He wrote. He did editorial work. He founded a publishing company and a few literary magazines, none of which were particularly successful. He lived a meager existence and published very little of consequence during most of his life. He earned some notoriety in Portugal two years before his death with the publication of a patriotic collection of poems called *The Message*. This could be the description of just about any writer who never quite made it, but Pessoa was not just any writer.

Besides the fame he gained with *The Message* at the end of his life, the other thing that was most interesting about Fernando Pessoa's otherwise unexceptional life was that he published under four different names: his own of course, as well as the name of Alberto Cairo, Álvaro de Campos, and Ricardo Reis.

Today, Pessoa is considered to be the greatest modern Portuguese poet, and arguably, the greatest Portuguese poet of all time. And perhaps even more remarkable, the other three poets—Alberto Cairo, Álvaro de Campos, and Ricardo Reis—who each wrote with a unique voice different from Pessoa's—would have also been recognized as world-class poets in their own right.

What was truly remarkable about Pessoa is that he wrote in what he called heteronyms, a term he invented. A pseudonym is an assumed name used by an author who chooses not to publish under their real name. But a heteronym is completely different, according to Pessoa. A heteronym is the name of an actual entity, a being, that wrote through Pessoa's body. Each of Pessoa's heteronyms has its own distinct body of work with a different writing style and focused on different content. The heteronyms even have detailed biographical histories and relationships between each other and with Pessoa.

Pessoa did not become globally recognized until decades after his death when his masterwork, *The Book of Disquiet,* was published posthumously in 1982. After his death at the age of forty-seven, a trunk was discovered containing over 25,000 items of unpublished writing. Among them were nineteen notebooks and thousands upon thousands of handwritten pages, some on napkins and scraps of paper, and none of which had been known to exist before. Suddenly, we learned that Fernando Pessoa, despite his infrequent publishing, had been writing volumes of material over the course of his life. The mystery of Fernando Pessoa deepened as scholars who explored the material of the trunk discovered many more than three heteronyms. In fact, they discovered that as many as 172 different people were writing through Pessoa.

The Book of Disquiet was pieced together from thousands of bits of material and is, in Pessoa's own words, a semi-fictional memoir. It was actually written by two people, but the heteronym that it is generally attributed to is Fernando Soares. Soares was an office clerk and lived a simple, solitary life. In the book, he drones on and on about the tedium of his existence and his love for the world of imagination. He appears to have had a profound spiritual awakening, the result of which, to some extent at least, was to increase his disdain for the world outside of imagination.

Fernando Pessoa, like Anaïs Nin, was very consciously creating a new art form and states so explicitly in *The Book of Disquiet*: "Let us create...art quite different from any other art" (21). Pessoa's new art, different from any other art, is the art of dreaming, which he describes in great detail in his book. Pessoa felt that his dreams were more real than the external world. In fact, what we all tend to call reality was for him nothing more than the dream we all agree to call real. Reality is no more real than any other dream. And for him, it was the dream he liked the least. He explored the art of dreaming like few ever have, and concluded that "The highest stage of dreaming is reached when having created a cast of characters, we live them all, all at the same time—we are all those souls jointly and interactively" (*The Book of Disquiet* 63). Fernando Pessoa was an Artist of Possibility, and the possibility that he was passionately dedicated to was perfecting the art of dreaming.

Pessoa had an interest in the occult and was acquainted with Aleister Crowley, the infamous English occultist. The two had met and bonded over their shared interest in astrology, and on one occasion, Crowley visited Pessoa in Lisbon. During this visit, they planned and staged Crowley's death. It seems that Crowley was so heartbroken over the fact that his consort had left him, that he asked Pessoa to publish articles in the Lisbon newspapers claiming that Crowley had flung himself to his death over the cliffs of a spot known as "Boca Do Inferno"—the Mouth of Hell. Word of Crowley's demise spread throughout the world—and would have stood indefinitely as the truth—except that, some months later, the occultist magician made a surprise appearance at one of his own art shows in Paris.

In regards to how his occultist leanings showed up in his writing, Pessoa insisted that the people that wrote through him were not pseudonyms, they were actual people—entities that would inhabit his body and write through him. Generally, when authors use pseudonyms, scholars who study them can still detect a distinctive style throughout their writing. But this does not appear to be true in Pessoa's case. His different heteronyms show up, even to scholars, as different individuals with different writing styles. And, when Pessoa wrote as these different individuals, the heteronyms felt completely different from him. As an example, when Pessoa wrote as himself, his writing process was incredibly labored. He worked hard at writing, edited and re-edited over and over again, and was seldom able to finish a piece to his satisfaction. But when Alberto Cairo wrote through him, it was always in a complete stream of consciousness style with very little, if any, editing at all. If William James had known of Fernando Pessoa, I imagine that a small contingent from the Psychical Research Society would have made the trip to Lisbon to study the obscure, yet fascinating poet.

We have already called Pessoa an Artist of Possibility and his passionate dedication to his writing gives evidence of the fact. Still, what was it that drove him? What was he so passionate about? With Nin, we saw that it was the quest for self-actualization that was driving her entire life. From my reading of Pessoa, I would say that the question of identity, of "Who am I?," seems to be that which burned within.

All through his writing, especially in *The Book of Disquiet*, Pessoa expresses doubts about his own existence. "I myself don't know if the 'I' I am setting before you in these serpentine pages really exists or is merely a false, self-created aesthetic concept of who I am" (36). He seems very confused about his existence, which, given how many people seemed to inhabit his writing process, is easy to imagine. Having so many other beings write through one person would naturally cause an identity crisis. His exploration of identity seems to have led to a climactic spiritual episode in which he experienced his own non-existence.

In my favorite passage from *The Book of Disquiet* he writes:

> In a moment of enlightenment, I realized that I am nobody, absolutely nobody...I, I myself am the center that exists only because the geometry of the abyss demands it. I am the nothing around which all this spins. I exist only so that it can spin. I am a center that exists only because every circle has one. (367)

Pessoa seems to see this realization of non-existence as the key to perfecting the art of dreaming:

> Because I am nothing, I can imagine myself to be anything. If I were somebody, I wouldn't be able to. An assistant bookkeeper can imagine himself to be a Roman emperor; the King of England can't do that, because the King of England has lost the ability in his dreams to be any other king than the one he is. His reality does not allow him to exist. (376)

Both Anaïs Nin's and Fernando Pessoa's lives seemed to be lived to serve their art. Nin lived a passionate and chaotic life because she believed that the "new psychological reality can be explored and dealt with only under the conditions of tremendously high atmospheric pressures, temperatures and speed..." (*Portable Anaïs Nin* 239). Pessoa, on the other hand, believed that the new art of dreaming could only be explored by someone who was nothing—someone who realized that they did not exist—and so, he lived a life that left him almost invisible to everyone, including himself. The possibilities that Nin and Pessoa were exploring could not be more diametrically opposed, yet their passionate commitment to devoting their entire lives to exploring them is identical. Artists of Possibility don't just make their art, they live it. But examining the lives of both Nin and Pessoa begs the question: does the artist's life create their art, or does their art create their life? The answer is probably both. The artist's life, and their art, are part of an artistic process of co-creation; the life of the artist shapes the art they create at the same time that the emerging art informs the artist on how to live.

In this chapter, we explored one of the passions of Artists of Possibility: the passionate surrender to a life of art. But before we conclude this discussion, I want to be sure that my choice of Nin and Pessoa to illustrate this deep passion doesn't leave you with the impression that Artists of Possibility are always writers. So, to close this chapter, I want to introduce you to the life and art of one more Artist of Possibility, the big wave surfer, Jeff Clark.

Jeff Clark was a seventeen-year-old high school student living on Miramar Beach in Half Moon Bay, California, when he made a discovery that would consume his life. Although his Northern California home was many miles from the epicenter of the California surfing community, the young Clark was passionate about the sport and spent many hours surfing the cold waters near his home on homemade surfboards. One day, he and a friend were looking at the huge breaking waves off the coast of Mavericks Beach. These waves were far out from the shore; you would need to swim half a mile just to reach them, but Clark wanted to go. One day, he decided it was time, but his friend declined to join, saying, "I will call the coast guard and tell them where I saw you last." Clark went out that day and surfed the monstrous wave that is now famously known as Mavericks and which has become a mecca for big wave surfers from around the world.

One of the most fascinating parts of Clark's story is that, even after he surfed the monster wave, he couldn't convince anyone to join him. It seemed that no one believed that such a huge wave, not to mention one that ended crashing into jagged rocks, could be surfed. For fifteen years, Jeff Clark surfed Mavericks all by himself. He went out day after day, swimming out the half-mile to catch the wave and risking his life riding what is still considered to be one of the most treacherous surf waves on earth. Clark describes one time when the wave pushed him under the surface and into the rocks. There was nothing he could do under such tremendous pressure except wait until the wave receded and hope he could make it to the surface before he drowned.

The wave did eventually recede so that Clark was able to swim to the surface, and after that, he kept right on surfing. He designed surfboards specifically to ride Mavericks. He trained himself to surf ambidextrously so he could ride it better. He tried to convince people to join him, but no one was willing to take him up on the offer until two surfers from Santa Cruz finally agreed to come. After their adventure at Mavericks, the two Santa Cruz surfers spread the news: California had a big wave to surf. Soon, there were cameras on the coast and big wave surfers coming from around the world to test their skill at Mavericks (*Riding Giants*).

Clark, like Nin and Pessoa, devoted his life to his art, the art of big wave surfing, and he created a possibility in Northern California that hadn't been there before. And, like Nin and Pessoa, he dedicated himself to it passionately without recognition for years. He was compelled to live his life for the wave and for the possibility of bringing it to the attention of the surfing world.

Artists of Possibility can work in any domain, because new possibilities are waiting to be created in philosophy as well as in surfing, in literature as much as in business, in science and in childcare. There is no aspect of human endeavor that doesn't have its Artists of Possibility pushing at the edges. And they aren't doing it for fame or money. So, what are they doing it for? What makes Artists of Possibility so compelled to manifest new possibilities? As we have said, they are simply called to it. They hear a possibility, and they can't say no.

CHAPTER 10

A School for Modern Mutants

MANY TIMES THROUGHOUT THIS BOOK, I have made reference to Gertrude Stein's definition of genius as "talking and listening at the same time" (*Lectures* 170). To me, that statement contains the essence of the process of art as John Dewey described it in *Art as Experience*; art emerges out of a process of mutual co-creation. In the last chapter, our explorations of Anaïs Nin and Fernando Pessoa revealed that the life of an artist was a reflection of the art they created and it is difficult to tell which created which. Did the artist's life create their art, or did the demands of their art create their life? This causal confusion is captured in the well-known question: which came first, the chicken or the egg? It is unavoidable, when examining the mutual co-creative process of art, to run into this question. It will always be impossible to tell which gave rise to the other because the question is premised on a false assumption, namely, that one thing had to come first.

The process of art cannot be limited to a linear succession of cause and effect through time. Neither can life itself be forced to fit neatly into a model of causal events happening along the straight line of time. This is part of what John Dewey was describing when he tried to debunk the idea of the reflex arc. It would be convenient for us if life could be completely explained in terms of one thing affecting another, and then that thing affecting the next and so on. A world governed only by linear cause and effect would remain comprehensible and predictable no matter how complex it got. Our minds have been shaped to see in terms of cause and effect, and so we project cause and effect on everything. But life, and art, are more complicated than that. They are not simply products of cause and effect; they are co-emergent phenomena. One doesn't appear first and then create the other. They emerge together, through a subtle and dynamic exchange of mutual influence.

In order to give you a visceral sense of what it means for two things to be co-emergent, I'd like to use the simple example of drawing a circle on paper. You start with a completely blank piece of white paper. You put your pen down on the paper somewhere and you draw a circle. Now, looking back at what you have done, you very plainly find a circle with an inside and an outside. Your act of drawing a circle on the paper simultaneously created an inside and an outside. Was it the inside of the circle that created the outside, or the outside that created the inside? The answer, of course, is neither. The inside and the outside of the circle both appeared simultaneously as the line of the circle was drawn. Similarly, the artist's life and their art emerge simultaneously as the art is formed. Anaïs Nin was not Anaïs Nin before she wrote her diaries, she became Anaïs Nin as her works were written, and just as importantly, as they were read. We are trained to see people as things with qualities—or, as we said earlier, as facts that we can be right or wrong about. But the truth is that people are not just things that have qualities, they are emergent phenomena that appear through the act of living.

The Artist of Possibility is aware of this, sometimes more consciously and explicitly, sometimes more unconsciously and implicitly. Either way, they relate to themselves as co-emergent with their art. They understand that they exist as a function of their art and the reception it receives. Of course, this is true for everyone. We are all co-emergent events, coming into being as we live our lives within the field of mutual influences that are constantly shaping us as we also affect them. The Artist of Possibility intuitively recognizes this and embraces the fact. This means that they see themselves not as active, independent agents willfully affecting the world around them, but rather as part of a larger creative process within which they play a miraculous, but far from all-powerful, role.

We could illustrate this by thinking about the difference between driving and sailing. When you drive a car, you use the energy and force of your motor to propel yourself down the highway. When you sail a boat, you are riding on the surface of an ocean propelled by the push of the wind in your sails. You do not need to generate your own power; you need to understand the powers that are affecting you and orient your sails to optimally harness those powers. You cannot go anywhere you want. The winds will move you in some directions, but not others. When driving a car, you generally feel separate from the road, but when sailing, it is almost impossible to feel separate from the ocean that carries you and the wind that pushes you along. Similarly, art—whether the art of writing, painting, philosophy, science, or big wave surfing—means finding your place in a process that is much larger than you. The bigger the embrace of the process, the bigger the potential of the art produced by it will be.

You have already learned a little bit about me and the artistry of possibility that I have been engaged with, which of course is and always will be an artwork in progress. After living a fairly conventional life, a series of spiritual experiences that I had—after coming into contact with a spiritual teacher and the community around him—compelled me to step out of my life and spend the next twenty years devoted to spiritual practice and awakening. My life is now committed to sharing the fruits of what I have and continue to discover. I cannot tell if my spiritual life created my spiritual work, or if my spiritual work created my spiritual life. I believe they simply co-emerged.

Through the course of this book, I have shared with you some of the life-altering events that occurred during one particular silent meditation retreat that I participated in. That retreat took place in June, July, and August of 2001, and I can say that, without a shadow of a doubt, the person who finished that retreat was not the same person that started it. The many reality-altering experiences I had during those sixty days, both on and off the meditation cushion, left me irrevocably open to a new world of possibility.

Three years later, I had another episode of spiritual awakening that I believe was the completion of what had begun there. The years immediately following the two-month retreat were a time of tremendous highs and devastating lows. There were some times when the universe herself, and all of her mysteries, seemed to open up to me like an oyster shell revealing the invaluable pearl of wisdom and love she held. And there were other times when I felt like I was wandering alone in a cold, dark night and it seemed impossible to know what was true, if anything. It is hard for me to know now how much of all this turmoil was part of an inevitable and unavoidable process of integrating into my life the massive shifts in consciousness that I had experienced on the retreat, and how much was generated by the imperfections of the spiritual situation I was in and the psychological blind spots of the teacher who headed it. I am sure both things were going on. But then, everything changed all over again, in December of 2005, when I was once again on a retreat, this time in Rishikesh, India.

I was sitting among 120 or so other retreatants listening to the teacher give a talk. I don't remember what the talk was about, but the content doesn't matter. As I listened intently, as I always did, my perspective flipped. I suddenly realized that the words coming out of the teacher's mouth were not his own. They were coming through him, but not from him. And when I looked around at all of the people listening with me in the audience, it suddenly became clear that our attention, interest, and focus were pulling the words out of the teacher's mouth and that the words were actually coming from somewhere beyond. What I saw all around me was the unfolding of a cosmic process of exchange. Information, realization, understanding, and insight, as well as all of the subtle emotions associated with them, were coming from the universe, through the speaker, and into the listeners.

Even more amazing was how clear it became to me that the rapt attention of the 120 people listening belonged to the very same cosmic being who was simultaneously offering wisdom through the speaker's mouth. The ears of the listeners and the voice of the speaker belonged to the same source of intelligence, and both were part of a higher-order process in which the universe was learning about itself. The genius of talking and listening at the same time was what was happening *all the time* in this universe. We had been trained to think that separate individuals were talking and listening to each other, but in this moment, I could see that it was all part of one co-emergent, evolving life form.

I knew immediately that I wanted to serve as a voice for that process to express itself to itself. After that retreat, I started teaching publicly in earnest. I began offering seminars, and soon, I was traveling throughout the world to share my enthusiasm for awakening and the mystical philosophy that supported it. I started a weekly internet radio program and a blog where I would write about the ideas that excited me.

Now, the question that I ask myself all the time is: How did all this happen? Why was I trying to escape my mind at such a young age? Why did I meet a spiritual teacher who would convince me to devote my life to awakening? What could possibly have given me the gumption to leave a perfectly good, normal life to join a very unconventional, and arguably unhealthy, spiritual community?

So many influences have shaped my life and my life's work; I could never claim credit for making it happen. If you look at it one way, it seems like a string of contingencies and chance events, but it feels to me like I was born to do all this and there is a reason behind it all that I cannot fathom. I feel it as it moves me through life. I am sailing on a sea of influences, and I believe there is a vast intelligence behind it all. My life has not always been easy—there have been times I was so low that I questioned whether I had the strength to go on—but I have also seen things I never could have dreamed of, and as a result, now live in a world where it seems that anything is possible.

As I look at my own life, it appears to me that it is created from patterns of influence that are too complex to understand, but which seem to be repeated in miniature in every part of my life. The writing of this book is a great example; writing this book has been an ongoing revelation of the same art of possibility that the book is about. Although I am only putting it down on paper now, this book has been writing itself throughout my entire life, at least since my early childhood spiritual explorations, and I feel certain that it started long before that.

One of the most fantastic illustrations of the art of possibility, and the uncanny merging of art and life that it can create, is found in the life and writings of the science-fiction author Philip K. Dick. Dick became a part of my life when I saw a movie based on one of his stories as a teenager, *Total Recall,* which revolves around a technology that allows you to purchase memory implants of a vacation. If you don't have time to go, or can't afford to, you can simply have a vacation memory implanted into your mind. "We'll remember it for you," the company's tagline states. But the obvious question raised is: "does it matter if the vacation you remember never actually happened?" (*Total Recall*).

As a teenager with a flair for the philosophical, I was hooked. And even now, as I write these words, I am actually listening to the soundtrack from the movie to help create the mood for what I am about to share.

Soon after watching *Total Recall*, I found another film based on a Philip K. Dick story, *Blade Runner*, in a video rental store. This time, the plot was centered on a near-future bounty hunter whose job it was to hunt human-like androids that had gone rogue and were posing as real humans. But, in this world, it is very difficult to discern these highly advanced androids from actual humans, and the bounty hunter begins to suspect that he himself might be a machine. The questions here, of course, are: "what is a human?" and "what makes someone real?" (*Blade Runner*).

My love for Philip K. Dick was sealed in stone. I'm pretty sure I have seen all of the movies based on his work by now, and have read a number of his novels.

Philip K. Dick's first novel was called *Gather Yourselves Together*. It was written in 1950 but wasn't published until 1994. The last novel he wrote was *The Transmigration of Timothy Archer*, published in 1982, the same year that he died. Between these two, Dick wrote 42 other novels and 121 short stories. Dick is famous for being a prolific writer, known to write all night, at times in an amphetamine-induced firestorm. His novels contain themes that were profoundly original when they were written, although some of them have become commonplace today. The questions he raised about the nature of reality, identity, memory, and society are so fresh in our own time, that movies and films are continually inspired by his stories. His writing is moody, paranoid, frightening, and yet beautifully mysterious and compelling. His stories seem to share more than the words can hold and more than what he was consciously intending. They feel pregnant with meaning. Dick was a prophetic visionary who lived a tragic and often painful life. "Absolute suffering leads to—is the means to—absolute beauty," Dick once wrote (*The Exegesis of Philip K. Dick* xi). And, like Nin and Pessoa, he seems to have consciously or unconsciously fashioned a life that proved it.

The moment that changed everything for Philip K. Dick occurred in February of 1974 when he, still groggy from the effects of medication administered during oral surgery earlier that day, answered the door to find a strikingly beautiful dark-haired girl standing there with a delivery of pain medication. The girl was wearing a necklace that featured the Christian symbol of a fish. This encounter with the fish necklace and the beautiful young woman initiated a series of intense spiritual episodes that seemed to download enormous amounts of information into Dick's nervous system (47-54).

Over the next eight years, Dick would write feverishly every night in an unending attempt to understand what had been given to him. At the time of his death in 1982, Dick would leave behind well over 8,000—mostly handwritten—pages containing what he called his *Exegesis*, his hermeneutical interpretation of not only his experience but also the hidden meanings behind all of his earlier writings.

Dick became convinced that, in his earlier novels, there was more being communicated than he had been aware of even while writing them. If it was true, then Dick had achieved the new novel writing that Anaïs Nin had been working on, which allowed him to express ideas beyond his conscious intentions. As part of his *Exegesis*, Dick began a systematic review of his earlier novels to uncover the secret messages that had been encoded into them without his knowing it.

The writing of the *Exegesis* makes Philip K. Dick a fascinating example of an Artist of Possibility because he was so obviously, and self-consciously, reinterpreting his own work. His books, originally written as stories, came to be recognized as storehouses of symbolic meaning that Dick came to believe had been inserted into him from a vast universal intelligence. Dick saw himself as playing a part in some immeasurable process of creative unfolding in which information vital to his own survival, and the future of our planet, was being revealed.

I originally found *The Exegesis of Philip K. Dick* in a small anarchist bookstore near my home in Philadelphia. Of course, being a fan, I picked up the 900-page tome and started reading the introduction. After reading for half an hour, I bought it. I found the book fascinating. It seemed to reveal the mind of a brilliant and disturbed genius. But of course, given Dick's extreme lifestyle and obvious personal failings, it would be easy to dismiss him as anything more than an unusually gifted literary talent who spent his life working in the marginalized outskirts of science-fiction.

Perhaps I never would have given more than my personal, and somewhat nostalgic, interest to *The Exegesis* if it hadn't been for one thing. Soon after buying it, I also picked up a copy of Jeffrey Kripal's book, *Mutants and Mystics* that included a discussion about Philip K. Dick and provided more intellectual context to consider him through.

The basic premise behind Jeffrey's wonderful book is that the world of the twentieth century became the world that William James feared it would, a world so completely dominated by the scientific paradigm and assumption of an objective factual reality that there is little, if any, room left for the reality of spiritual or paranormal possibilities. There is simply no way left to express your spiritual experiences that won't make you look crazy in most people's eyes. But, of course, people don't stop having spiritual revelations just because society no longer believes in them. So, people either keep them to themselves—sometimes to the extreme of forgetting about them altogether—or they find a new venue to express them in disguise.

In *Mutants and Mystics*, Jeffrey shows us how many spiritual and paranormal experiences find their way into the pages of fantastic fiction and comic books. He looks at these works, published over the course of the twentieth century, and finds what he calls a super-story. As I understand it, what Jeffrey means by a super story is an overarching cultural narrative that an entire society lives through. These super stories show up in cultural artifacts like music, literature, movies and comic books. The super-story that Jeffrey is illuminating in *Mutants and Mystics* contains seven sub-themes, which Jeffrey traces through the decades of the Twentieth Century.

Over the past few years, my growing respect for and friendship with Jeffrey has been a source of tremendous positive influence on my work. Through him, I saw that my early love of comic books and pulp science fiction was driven by my sensitivity to the super-stories that wanted to write their way into our world. As Jeffrey sees it, these stories want to enter our world, and when they find a writer or an artist sensitive to them, they inspire them to create. But the resulting creations are not the product of the author alone; the super-story that wants to manifest speaks itself to and through the writer as the writer imagines the story. The writer's imagination is certainly at work in the process, but the writer is not making the story up either. They are being given a story in a raw, unwritten form which they then put into words.

This context helps me to understand and sympathize with Philip K. Dick. He seems to have had a direct interaction with some aspect of the super-story that was writing itself through his novels, or perhaps it was his angelic other half. Either way, he very consciously realized that he had been part of a larger process of creation during his entire career. For the next eight years, he couldn't stop working on his *Exegesis*, desperate to understand what was going on. Perhaps, emotionally and psychologically, Dick was not prepared for the challenge of that realization. Perhaps a super-story, which we could also think of as a higher-dimensional being, will work itself through any receptive and sensitive vessel, regardless of their readiness for the task.

I want to remind you that Jeffrey Kripal is a serious academic scholar of comparative religions and that my interest in science-fiction and comic books was mostly enjoyed in my youth, and only occasionally in my adult life. But one of the things that I find so admirable and exhilarating about his work is how he so convincingly shows that the world of mysticism and spiritual awakening is connected to the world of fantasy, comic books, and the paranormal. In days when religion still held a central place of esteem in the world, it was safer to express spiritual experiences as our own, actual experiences without needing to write them into the stories of our fictional superheroes.

But Jeffrey's exploration of spiritual super-stories is not limited to fiction. More recently, in a conversation with him, I found out that he had written his doctoral thesis on another of the great Hindu mystics, the nineteenth-century revered saint from Kolkata, Ramakrishna. Although, as I have already discussed, my years of spiritual practice followed the tradition of Ramana Maharshi, in the years since my former community disbanded I have come to realize a deep affinity to Ramakrishna.

Ramana Maharshi and Ramakrishna are both revered saints of India, but their manifestation of divinity is very different. Ramana, as we have said, lay down at the age of sixteen to see what it would be like to die, and then, realizing that consciousness survives even after death, abandoned his worldly life. For some time, he refused to engage with the world in any way, refusing even to eat unless his devotees fed him. Later, he did become involved with daily life at his ashram, but seemed to have lived in a simple, quiet, and devoted way, teaching his practice of self-inquiry and the Hindu philosophy of Advaita Vedanta.

Ramakrishna had his first experience of spiritual ecstasy, in which he became completely absorbed in an inner state of supreme joy, at age six. Ramakrishna would experience states of ecstatic absorption frequently throughout his life. Sometimes those states would result in prolonged periods of silence, but other times he would break out into wild song and dance. Ramakrishna was a devotee of the divine mother, and expressing his love for her was his primary passion. Ramakrishna would eventually become a temple priest where he engaged in tremendous amounts of spiritual practice in the hopes that the goddess Kali would reveal herself to him. He became so desperate in his efforts that he decided to kill himself and ran for a sword that was hanging on the temple wall, intending to throw himself upon it. But just before he reached the sword, he was overcome with a vision of Kali. His prayers had been answered.

Eventually, Ramakrishna's family became worried that all the intense spiritual practice was destabilizing him, and they arranged for him to be married so he could settle down into a normal life. His home with his wife became a temple of sorts that attracted daily guests from all over India who wished to see and learn from the revered saint.

Ramakrishna was always consumed by his love for the divine in all her forms. He is said to have mastered the practices of Tantra as well as those of Advaita Vedanta. He also became a realized adept of both Islamic and Christian mystical practices. He was an early pioneer of interfaith dialog and had an unending stream of devotees coming constantly to his home. One devotee that he loved in particular would come to see him often, and they would sit together in the rapture of shared God-intoxication. They would simply peer into each other's eyes and see the vast reaches of the unending inner cosmos. Their love was so deep that some in their circles even expressed misgivings about it.

The young devotee's name was Narendra and, in time, he would become a great teacher himself. In fact, he eventually made a long and arduous journey to America without a penny to his name. He arrived with a new title, Swami Vivekananda, and spoke at the first Parliament of the World's Religions held in Chicago in 1893. The presentation he gave at the Parliament is the stuff of legend. He spoke with such poise and grace, effortlessly explaining the most sublime spiritual truths while displaying the learned qualities of a truly sophisticated man. The audience was intoxicated by this man dressed in strange robes who had traveled so far with no money. The spirituality of the East had truly arrived in the West.

My point in introducing both Ramakrishna and Philip K. Dick in this chapter is that, if you examine the details of Dick's spiritual revelations and explore the accounts of the ecstasies of Ramakrishna, you find more similarities than differences. Both of them experienced intense periods of inner vision, they were both certain that they had been directly in contact with an all-knowing, higher being, and they were both obsessed with a need to understand the nature of that being and the message they had been given for the world. They even seemed to share some self-destructive tendencies.

However, in pointing out these similarities, I definitely do not want to equate Philip K. Dick, an avant-garde science-fiction writer, with Ramakrishna, one of the most revered saints of India. There were many differences between them that are beyond the scope of this book to explore. Of course, there is the fact that Ramakrishna's first revelations happened in early childhood and Dick's toward the end of this life. But there is one other obvious difference that I do want to point out: Ramakrishna grew up in the religious world of nineteenth-century India, while Philip K. Dick lived in the secular world of mid-twentieth-century America.

Although Ramakrishna's family was very worried about him and his spiritual fits, and he was considered to be dangerously insane by others, he lived in a context within which it was possible for some people to recognize his eccentricities as spiritual gifts and revelations. He was given a job as a priest in a temple and built a large and devoted following because of his powerful spiritual episodes. In spite of the misgivings of some, there were many who interpreted Ramakrishna's visions and behaviors in a religious context. His experiences were publicly validated and respected by many, and he was materially supported as a result of having them.

Philip K. Dick, on the other hand, literally lived the life of a starving artist. Dick discusses the hardship of his life in an introductory essay to his book *The Golden Man*. The essay was called "The Lucky Pet Store" and it opens with these words, "When I see these stories of mine, written over three decades, I think of the Lucky Dog Pet Store. There's a good reason for that. It has to do with an aspect of not just my life but with the lives of most free-lance writers. It's called poverty" (*Shifting Realities* 84).

The essay, written after he was fifty years old, is a nostalgic trip back in time to the self-destructive life of poverty that he led for a long time. The essay hinges on the fact that he and his wife at the time would buy some of their food at the pet shop because it was all they could afford. He was an artist, a writer, and evidently an extraordinary one, but he lived in a society in which artists did not garner much public recognition, at least not until they became famous. I suppose that was the catch-22 of the situation; famous artists were revered and unknown artists were ignored, but all artists started as unknowns. There was little general recognition of artists and very little structural support to assist them while they developed their craft.

In those days of poverty, Dick found solace in the circle of science-fiction writers. In his essay, he mentions Harlan Ellison, A. E. van Vogt, Theodore Sturgeon, Roger Zelazny, Norman Spinrad, and Thomas Disch as members of his circle—a veritable who's who of science-fiction writers of the time. "The loneliness of the writing per se is offset by the fraternity of writers," he wrote (87).

Artists of Possibility need to be supported. One of the important points I have been making in this book is that we do not live in a world of things that have qualities and characteristics inherent in themselves. Reality is not a set of objective facts waiting to be discovered. Reality is interpreted; it is read like a book and people are, too. We are not something that pops into the world ready-made. We become someone through the profound and subtle interaction of influences that mutually affect one another into existence. Yes, Ramakrishna had a rare and profound spiritual gift and, in the context of nineteenth-century India, he became a revered saint—sometimes said to be as significant as the Buddha. Philip K. Dick also had profound spiritual gifts, but in the context of twentieth-century America, he found little support.

This was part of what William James feared would happen. He saw that modern society was heading in a direction in which anything that was not objectively observable and measurable would be neglected, devalued, and dismissed. He felt that the paranormal gifts of people like Leonora Piper needed to be taken seriously because they offered untold value to the world. He worked hard throughout his life, risking his career and his reputation to carve out a place of legitimacy for those things that were spiritual but not religious.

Jeffrey Kripal came to some notoriety as a religious scholar when he published *Esalen: America and the Religion of No Religion*, a nearly 600-page history of the now-famous center for human potential founded by Michael Murphy and Dick Price in Big Sur, California, in 1962. In his book, Jeffrey compares Esalen to the school for mutants run by Professor Xavier in the popular *X-Men* comics. He describes Esalen as "...an esoteric or alternative academy where the human potentialities of mystical and psychical experience could be protected, educated, disciplined, and eventually stabilized within a set of transformative practices" (*Esalen* 109).

I would love to be able to bring William James to Esalen and show him around. I can see him standing with his hands on his hips shouting out to no one in particular, "You see, I told you to keep your minds open!"

I consider myself to be extremely fortunate. When I found the spiritual community that would become my home for two decades, the thing that

I was attracted to most was the community. The idea of being able to explore awakening with like-minded souls was so attractive that I gave up my entire life for it. And I am even luckier because I feel that I fared well in an environment that could have been harmful. Through it all, I am now able to make a living sharing the fruits of my spiritual life with the many people who come to me seeking guidance and support. In my own way, I have built and continue to build a context that recognizes the value of our spiritual sensitivities. We need these gathering places to incubate our capacities for creative illumination. Those of us who find that we are open to new possibilities too often find ourselves in a world where we have to dim our light to fit in. A big part of my intention in writing this book is to recognize the value of those many, many people who have experienced, and continue to experience, new possibilities for this world. In my own way, I am creating a context to support the emergence of Artists of Possibility.

CHAPTER 11

The Possibility That's Already Living Within You

MY LIFE HAS BEEN DEVOTED to a possibility that called to me from beyond time and space. This possibility emerges through me from a place that cannot be cognized. It is an other-dimensional potential. Whatever it is, it was the energy behind my birth. I feel as if I was pushed into existence to reveal a very specific possibility, to give it shape and form in the world. I believe you were too. You were born from a place beyond imagination to give shape to a possibility that literally pushed you into existence and has been living through you from the very beginning. If you think about it, you probably already know this somewhere deep inside yourself.

Many times, people will come to me and ask something like, "I know I am here for something greater, but I don't know what it is. How do I find my purpose? Where do I look to see the possibility that is trying to live through me?"

What you need to realize is that the possibility that wants to live through you is not hiding from you. Or if it is hiding, it is hiding in plain sight. Where? In the life you're already living.

In my own case, I can see that possibility in my early childhood experiences in my father's locked car, then in summer evenings laying on the ground staring up into the night sky. Eventually, I studied physics as an undergraduate and became a self-proclaimed and outspoken atheist. (Well, I was only outspoken with my father on Sunday mornings to justify why I wasn't going to church.) In my senior year of college, I took two semesters of quantum mechanics and learned about the then-popular string theory of reality. I lost my faith in physics. String theory seemed, to me, to be a story that scientists were making up to explain the unexplainable, no less so than any religious story. Ernst Mach would have been proud, I think. Now, string theory has largely fallen out of favor, which I see as a testament to the integrity of science—but it was too late for me, I started looking for a new path of discovery.

I began studying cognitive science because I became convinced that our relationship with our mind must hold the key to reality. Cognitive science introduced me to the mysterious ways that we create our experience of reality through a complex, mostly unconscious, process of filtration and interpretation. It also led me to the practice of meditation, in an initially secular context.

My search for meditation instruction led me to a weekend at a Hindu ashram in Upstate New York, then to a Sufi center in Boston, and finally to a Buddhist meditation center in Cambridge. Somewhere along the way, I came across a book by a Catholic monk named Thomas Merton. That book, *New Seeds of Contemplation*, became my bible, and Merton became my first spiritual teacher.

Thomas Merton's biography, *The Seven Story Mountain*, was published in 1948. Its original print run was 7,500 copies, but pre-publication sales hit 20,000 orders. The original hardcover edition eventually sold 600,000 copies. Evidently, there was something about Merton's story of religious conversion and the inner fruits of the monastic life that a lot of people wanted to read about. Once I started reading Merton, I couldn't get enough. Soon I was taking a class offered at a monastery. The class, on the life and writings of Thomas Merton, took place in a classroom that was big enough to hold about forty students, but which we occupied each week with only fifteen. Along the back wall were about twelve monks dressed in robes, who I believe were residents at the monastery, while in the forty or so desks, were three people, me and two nuns in habits.

Each week, I was more and more amazed at what I was learning. Merton's story, starting with his birth in Europe to bohemian artist parents, followed by his conversion to Catholicism and his decision to become a monk, spoke deeply to me. Merton's call to a life of spiritual integrity and authenticity gripped me. In *New Seeds of Contemplation*, the chapter called "Integrity" begins with these lines:

Many poets are not poets for the same reason that many religious men are not saints: they never succeed in being themselves. They never get around to being the particular poet or the particular monk they are intended to be by God. They never become the man or the artist who is called for by all the circumstances of their individual lives. (14)

I never forgot these lines. I didn't know what God intended for me, but I knew that I wanted to become that. I didn't know what it was, or why, but I knew there was a reason I was here. Thomas Merton taught me about the necessity of following your own vocation.

Self-actualization means becoming the artist, the mother, the banker, the writer, the athlete, or the entrepreneur that divinity, your higher Self, or your angelic other half, is calling you to be. Don't adopt anyone else's path as your own. Don't imitate. Discover who you are, and be yourself. There is only one right path for you, and it's yours. It won't necessarily look like the one you imagined, it won't look like your neighbor's, and it probably won't look like your hero's either. It is your own unique expression of a very particular vision of possibility that was given only to you.

I believe with all my heart that you are being lived by a possibility. You may already know that, or you may just be realizing it now, but either way, there is something that wants to manifest through you. It is coming from a place beyond imagination, and it can only come through you as you engage in a co-creative process in which you discover it and create it at the same time.

It's very possible that you already know more about what is living through you than you remember. You may have known what you were here for once, and then forgotten about it.

Something happened on the forty-eighth day of the same meditation retreat that transformed my life, after the awakening of Kundalini and the nights of constant consciousness. At this stage in the retreat, my meditation had become consistently effortless. I would just sit and let everything be as it is, and I would allow the miracles of reality to reveal themselves to me. But on this particular day, during one of the meditation sessions, I started to feel a sense of expansion. It was something I had been feeling fairly regularly over the last few weeks, but this time, it was different. I actually felt myself physically expanding. I was moving upward, closer to the ceiling and further from the floor. I sat quietly, relaxed deeply, and let it happen. I had become accustomed to bizarre experiences and wasn't startled at all.

Eventually, my line of site approached the ceiling and I was ready to feel my head bump up against it. Instead, my eyesight passed right through it. I saw a cross-section of the ceiling go by and then I was outside, above the roof. I could see the trees around the building as I kept moving higher and higher upward. I rose above the trees and could see the buildings in the town below me. Soon, the nearby lake was just a small part of a landscape that was now far away from me. I just sat and let it all happen.

At some point, I could see the entire sphere of the earth below me. Then, I was way out in space and I couldn't identify the earth anymore from the stars in the sky. I kept expanding and expanding until, eventually, the expansion slowed to a halt. My body was the entire universe. I was all there was. I was experiencing cosmic consciousness. I felt a profound sense of satisfaction and completion. It was like an infinite sigh of relief. I was home. I felt a love bigger than anything I had ever known before.

At that moment, I also remembered something very vividly. I remembered that I had done exactly this when I was a very small child. I remembered being very young and going into the bathroom of my parent's house. There was a full-length mirror on the back of the door. I would lock the door behind me and stare into my eyes until I would feel myself expand up through the roof of the house. I would keep expanding until I was so big that when I looked down my whole body was the universe. I would feel that same deep sense of satisfaction, relief, and love. Then I would gradually allow myself to shrink down to my normal size, unlock the bathroom door, and go about my business. I couldn't have been more than four years old. I vaguely remembered doing this often but remembered very distinctly how, one time, I looked at myself in the bathroom mirror, stared into my eyes, and realized that I couldn't do it anymore. I couldn't expand. I remembered feeling deeply sad and depressed about this. I had lost my access to the imaginal realm and my portal to the divine beyond.

I was thirty-seven years old when I went on the two-month retreat. I had completely forgotten about the most important part of my life for around thirty-three years. But now that I remembered it, everything made sense. It was obvious what I had been looking for inside my father's car, staring into the night sky, and living in a spiritual community. I had come into this life with a secret and I had forgotten it so completely that I didn't even remember that something was missing. Still, there was a part of me that never gave up trying to remember what it was.

A few years ago, I was leading a retreat and I told this story. I asked people to pair with a partner and try to remember any spiritual experiences that they might have forgotten. A number of people had a forgotten experience return to them, but one man's experience was particularly powerful. He was about seventy years old and had been attending meditation retreats for decades. He always claimed that he'd never had a spiritual experience, which I found hard to believe. He must have had some experience, I reasoned, or he wouldn't do so many retreats. After the dialogue exercise, he was very excited to share something that he remembered. When he was twenty-two, he had had a mind-blowing awakening experience. It had shaken him at his core, but he had no context to help him understand it. It was the first time in nearly fifty years that he had remembered. He was beaming, radiating as he spoke. Suddenly, his decades of spiritual search made sense to him in a new way.

How many profound spiritual experiences might you have had and forgotten about so completely that you don't even realize that there is anything to remember? I believe they are there, and when you remember them, you will see various encounters you've had with your angelic other half.

To bring this book to a close, I have an admission to make. For years, I had thought of Thomas Merton as my first spiritual teacher, but more recently—and in light of my early experiences of cosmic consciousness—I have realized that I had a teacher before Merton, who was the most important of all. My first spiritual teacher was Captain Marvel, the comic book superhero from the 1970s.

I would have been nine years old when *Captain Marvel* "Issue #29" hit stands in 1973. I remember the cover of the issue perfectly because I would spend hours drawing it over and over again. Captain Marvel was depicted with his arms outstretched, flying overhead across the starry background of the cosmos. I didn't remember the story, probably because I was too young to understand most of it, but I was transfixed by that comic book. Captain Marvel was my favorite superhero. I had no idea at the time why, and I certainly didn't realize that I had had a spiritual transformation from the story in "Issue #29," but I read through the story again just this morning and it's crystal clear now that Captain Marvel, "the most cosmic superhero of all," was my first spiritual teacher.

Captain Marvel "Issue #29" ends with a battle against a villain known as the Controller. The battle goes badly for Captain Marvel, and he finds himself buried alive under a mountain of rubble and, even worse, transformed back into his human self, Rick Jones. It looks as if he will certainly perish. Suddenly, the scene shifts and Captain Marvel finds himself on the surface of a strange planet being confronted by a being called Eon who is depicted as a large face, floating against a cosmic background. He has a huge soul's eye that reminds me now of the all-seeing, transparent eyeball of Ralph Waldo Emerson.

Eon commands Captain Marvel to stare into the soul's eye so that he can tell him why he is here. According to the comic book, Eon has been waiting for the arrival of Captain Marvel since before the birth of Olympus. Eon relays the story of a fallen Greek god who arranged for a hero to arrive at the right moment to protect the cosmos from the evil Thanos. Captain Marvel is that hero, and now is that time, but he must undergo an inner transformation in order to become the hero he was born to be. Captain Marvel must see beyond his own violent ways and defeat the inner ravagers who want to destroy his dreams. Finally, he must banish his inner demon. Only when these inner battles have been won can Eon give Captain Marvel the gift that he has waited an eternity to give.

Captain Marvel makes one last plea to Eon. "...why are you doing this to me?" he calls out.

"Because you must see..." says Eon, who then takes Captain Marvel on a journey through his past, explaining that he has "lived and accepted the ways of the warrior!" But that "the universe now needs not a warrior, but a protector!"

Captain Marvel is ready. "I wish to change," he says.

"With the wish comes the reality!" Eon says, but ".... the mental change has to come from within!"

Captain Marvel defeats the ravagers, and in battling his inner demon, has a life-transforming realization. "To live is to strive! To strive is to seek! In this sphere of existence only one thing is worth seeking, that which gives life meaning...FREEDOM!"

"Our cosmic opera is completed!" Eon then declares, "You now stand ready to fulfill a destiny charted billions of light-years ago!"

"Issue #29" ends with an iconic image of Captain Marvel's face. Shown only in silhouette, his countenance has been replaced with an image of the starry cosmos. The gift of cosmic consciousness has been bestowed upon him (Starlin 110-128).

Captain Marvel was my first spiritual teacher. He taught me about inner and cosmic purpose. Although I didn't remember my childhood experiences of when I read that issue, something in me remembered, and I was propelled more fully onto the path that would eventually result in a re-awakening of cosmic consciousness and my current life as a meditation teacher and mystical philosopher.

I came into this life with a memory of cosmic consciousness but then forgot about it. It was as if I had emerged at birth from an unimaginable, unitive wholeness and then lost touch with that majesty as my mind became structured by logical principles, exactly the way Benjamin Paul Blood and William James experienced their returns from nitrous oxide inebriation. Years later, I was drawn to Captain Marvel because the images of his cosmic face stirred an unconscious memory of my true Self. This awakened the energy of genius and spurred the search that would drive my entire life.

But that way of looking at it doesn't feel quite right to me. It feels too linear, too defined by cause and effect. What feels more accurate to me is that the possibility that I was born to serve is not emerging through my life linearly, one moment after the next; it arises through my whole life all at once—now. It is coming up right now in my life as a three-year-old in the bathroom expanding into cosmic awareness. It is coming up in my father's car and lying on my back gazing up at the stars. It is emerging in the classroom where I learn about Thomas Merton. And, of course, it is visible as I make the unprecedented decision to leave my life and join a spiritual community and while I sit in meditation during the two-month retreat. All of this is emerging in the eternal *now*, simultaneously, as I type these words.

The possibility that is living through me is connected to the possibilities that are emerging through the lives of William James, Gertrude Stein, Anaïs Nin, Ramana Maharshi, and everyone else who has inspired and guided me along the way, including you, right now, as you read these words. You are pulling this book out of me as you read. You are completing it by adding your interpretation to it.

Many possibilities are emerging into being right now, and they are all happening simultaneously, everywhere. This living, present moment is thick with possibilities. If you stare into it, you will see that there are possibilities upon possibilities all coexisting right now, and one of them is looking back at you. It is calling you to live it. Its contours can be seen by looking at your life and putting together the puzzle pieces of all the times that it has spoken to you most clearly. And as you unravel the story of your own art of possibility, you will discover the story that has been living through your life since before you were born.

In this book, I have attempted to share a way of seeing that allows you to recognize who you are and see the gift you are here to give. That is the art of possibility. It reveals the story you came to live. It is the possibility that wants to be born through you. It is living and being lived at the same time. The life of an Artist of Possibility can be a lonely one; there are too few of us around with too little support in the world. So, this book is an offer of food for your soul as you walk your path. I hope it gives you the comfort that comes from knowing you are not alone.

If you have ever felt that you were here for something bigger, I want you to know that you were right. You are here to give birth to a possibility that is bigger than you can imagine, but at the same time, it is nothing more than the full expression of who you already are.

Works Cited

Bailey, Jeffrey. "Anaïs Nin: Link in the Chain of Feeling." New Orleans Review. https://www.neworleansreview.org/anais-nin-link-in-the-chain-of-feeling/. Accessed 27 Oct. 2020.

Bakewell, Sarah. At the Existentialist Café: Freedom, Being and Apricot Cocktails. Chatto & Windus, 2016.

Barrett, William. *Irrational Man: A Study in Existential Philosophy.* Anchor Books, 2011.

Berlin, Isaiah. *The Roots of Romanticism,* edited by Henry Hardy, Princeton University Press, 2001.

Blade Runner. Directed by Ridley Scott, performances by Sean Young, Harrison Ford, and Rutger Hauer, Warner Brothers, 1982.

Blum, Deborah. *Ghost Hunters: William James and the Search for Scientific Proof of Life after Death.* Penguin Books, 2007.

Bordogna, Francesca. *William James at the Boundaries: Philosophy, Science, and the Geography of Knowledge.* The University of Chicago Press, 2008.

Breen, Benjamin. "Extreme, Extreme!" *The Paris Review,* 17 Sept. 2014. https://www.theparisreview.org/blog/2014/09/17/extreme-extreme/.

Bucke, Richard Maurice. *Cosmic Consciousness: A Study in the Evolution of the Human Mind.* Penguin Compass, 1991.

Cahn, Aisha. *A Journey from Me to You.* Balboa Press, 2018.

Cheetham, Tom. *All the World an Icon: Henry Corbin and the Angelic Function of Beings.* North Atlantic Books, 2012.

Coleridge, Samuel Taylor. *Aids to Reflection and the Confessions of an Inquiring Spirit.* London, 1825.

Cone, Michèle C. "The Steins Collect: An Irreverent Report." *Artnet,* 7 Mar. 2012, https://www.academia.edu/10219172/THE_STEINS_COLLECT_AN_IRREVERENT_REPORT.

Cooke, George Willis. *Ralph Waldo Emerson: His Life, Writings, and Philosophy.* 2nd ed., Boston, 1882.

Cott, Jonathan. "Henry Miller: Reflections of a Cosmic Tourist: An aternoon with the celebrated author." *Rolling Stone,* February 27, 1975, https://www.rollingstone.com/culture/culture-features/henry-miller-reflections-of-a-cosmic-tourist-171175/.

da Silva, Jorge Bastos, and Joana Matos Frias. *A Time to Reason and Compare: International Modernism Revisited One Hundred Years After.* Cambridge Scholars Publishing, 2016.

Dewey, John. *Art as Experience.* Perigee, 1980.

Dewey, John. *Experience and Nature.* Dover Publications, 2000.

Dewey, John. *Human Nature and Conduct.* Dover, 2012.

Dick, Philip K. *The Exegesis of Philip K. Dick,* edited by Pamela Jackson and Jonathan Lethem, Houghton Mifflin Harcourt, 2011.

Dick, Philip K. *Ubik.* Mariner Books, 2012.

Dick, Philip K. *Valis.* Mariner Books, 2011.

Dick, Philip K. "'Introduction' to The Golden Man (1980)." *The Shifting Realities of Philip K. Dick: Selected Literary and Philosophical Writings,* edited by Lawrence Sutin, Vintage Books, 1996, pp. 84-96.

Emerson, Ralph Waldo. *Essay & Lectures,* edited by Joel Porte, Library of America, 1983.

Emerson, Ralph Waldo. *Natural History of the Intellect,* Wrightwood Press, 2008.

Fitch, Noel Riley. *Sylvia Beach and the Lost Generation: A History of Literary Paris in the Twenties and Thirties.* W.W. Norton Company, 1985.

Folgarait, Leonard. *Painting 1909.* Yale University Press, 2017.

Frederick, Norris. "William James and Swami Vivekananda: Religious Experience and Vedanta/Yoga in America." *William James Studies,* vol. 9, 2012, pp. 37-55. https://williamjamesstudies.org/wp-content/uploads/2014/03/frederick.pdf.

Grieve-Carlson, Timothy. "The Methodologies of Radical Empiricism: The Experiential Worlds of William James and Carles Fort." *Academia,* https://

www.academia.edu/39412894/The_Methodologies_of_Radical_
Empiricism_The_Experiential_Worlds_of_William_James_and_
Charles_Fort_Timothy_Grieve_Carlson. Accessed August 29, 2020.

Guy, David, and H. P. Blavatsky. "The Mysterious Madame B." *Tricycle Magazine*,
1996, https://tricycle.org/magazine/mysterious-madame-b/.

Hemingway, Ernest. *A Moveable Feast.* Restored ed., Scribner, 2009.

Hixon, Lex. *Great Swan: Meetings with Ramakrishna.* Shambhala, 1992.

James, William. The Varieties of Religious Experience: A Study in Human
Nature. Routledge, 2008.

James, William. *Writings 1878-1899.* Library of America, 1992.

James, William. Writings 1902-1910. Library of America, 1988.

James, William. "Review of 'The Anaesthetic Revelation and the Gist of
Philosophy.'" The Atlantic. Nov. 1874. https://www.theatlantic.com/past/
docs/issues/96may/nitrous/wmjgist.htm.

James, William. "Subjective Effects of Nitrous Oxide." *Carnegie Mellon University
School of Computer Science.* http://www.cs.cmu.edu/~ehn/release/nitrous.
html. Accessed 25 Sept. 2020.

James, William. "The Energies of Men." *Science*, vol. 25, no. 635, 1 Mar. 1907, pp.
321-332, https://www.jstor.org/stable/1632253.

James, William. "The Hidden Self." *Wiki Source.* https://en.wikisource.org/wiki/
The_Hidden_Self. Accessed 25 Sept. 2020.

John, Da Free. *The Four Fundamental Questions: Talks and essays about human
experience and the actual practice of an Enlightened Way of Life.* Dawn Horse
Press, 1980.

Kandinsky, Wassily. *Concerning the Spiritual in Art.* Translated by M. T. H. Sadler,
Dover Publications, 1977.

Knapp, Krister Dylan. *William James: Psychical Research and the Challenge of
Modernity.* The University of North Carolina Press, 2017.

Kripal, Jeffrey J. *Esalen: America and the Religion of No Religion.* The University of
Chicago Press, 2007.

Kripal, Jeffrey J. *Kālī's Child: The Mystical and the Erotic in the Life and Teachings of*

Ramakrishna. 2nd ed., University of Chicago Press, 1998.

Kripal, Jeffrey J. *Mutants & Mystics: Science Fiction, Superhero Comics, and the Paranormal*. University of Chicago Press, 2011.

Krizan, Kim. *Spy in the House of Anaïs Nin.* Total Global Domination, 2019.

Krohn, Elizabeth G, and Jeffrey J. Kripal. *Changed in a Flash: One Woman's Near-Death Experience and Why a Scholar Thinks it Empowers Us All*. North Atlantic Books, 2018.

Kuhn, Thomas S. *The Structure of Scientific Revolutions*. Enlarged 2nd ed., University of Chicago Press, 1990.

Lachman, Gary. *Lost Knowledge of the Imagination*. Floris Books, 2017.

Lehrer, Jonah. "Gertrude Stein: The Structure of Language." *Proust Was a Neuroscientist*. Mariner Books, 2008, pp. 144-167.

Levy, Deborah. "How a book by Gertrude Stein taught me to write about myself." *The Guardian*. 13 Apr. 2020, https://www.theguardian.com/commentisfree/2020/apr/13/book-gertrude-stein-autobiography-alice-b-toklas.

Lubow, Arthur. "An Eye for Genius: The Collections of Gertrude and Leo Stein." *Smithsonian Magazine*, Jan. 2012, https://www.smithsonianmag.com/arts-culture/an-eye-for-genius-the-collections-of-gertrude-and-leo-stein-6210565/.

Mach, Ernst. *The Analysis of Sensation, and the Relation of the Physical to the Psychical*. Translated by C. M. Williams, 5th ed., Open Court Publishing, 1914.

Maharshi, Ramana. *The Spiritual Teaching of Ramana Maharshi*. Shambhala, 2004.

Mead, George H. *Mind, Self, and Society: From the Standpoint of A Social Behaviorist*, edited by Charles W. Morris, vol. 1, University of Chicago Press, 1967.

Mellow, James R. *Charmed Circle: Gertrude Stein & Company*. Praeger, 1974.

Menand, Louis. *The Metaphysical Club*. Farrar, Straus and Giroux, 2002.

Merton, Thomas. *Echoing Silence: Thomas Merton on the Vocation of Writing*, edited by Robert Inchausti, New Seeds, 2007.

Merton, Thomas. *New Seeds of Contemplation*. New Directions, 2007.

Meyer, Steven. *Irresistible Dictation: Gertrude Stein and the Correlations of Writing and Science*. Stanford University Press, 2002.

Monet, Claude. *Rouen Cathedral, West Facade, Sunlight*. 1894, The Met, New York.

Newton, Isaac. "Four Letters to Doctor Bentley." Sophia Rare Books, 19 Oct. 2020. https://www.sophiararebooks.com/pages/books/3537/ sir-isaac-newton/four-letters-to-doctor-bentley.

Nikhilananda, Swami, translator. *The gospel of Sri Ramakrishna*. By Sri Ramakrishna, Ramakrishna-Vivekananda Center, 1942.

Nin, Anaïs. *D. H. Lawrence: An Unprofessional Study*. Swallow Press, 1964.

Nin, Anaïs. *Delta of Venus*. Houghton Mifflin Harcourt, 1977.

Nin, Anais. *Incest: The Unexpurgated Diary of Anaïs Nin*. Houghton Mifflin Harcourt, 1992.

Nin, Anais. *The Diary of Anaïs Nin, Vol. 1: 1931-1934*. Houghton Mifflin Harcourt, 1966.

Nin, Anaïs. *The Portable Anaïs Nin*. Edited by Benjamin V. Franklin. Sky Blue Press, 2010.

Noë, Alva. *Varieties of Presence*. Harvard University Press, 2012.

Osborne, Arthur. *The Mind of Ramana Maharshi*. Jaico Publishing House, 1959.

Perry, Ralph Barton. *The Thought and Character of William James*. Harper Torchbooks, 1964.

Pessoa, Fernando. *A Little Larger Than the Entire Universe: Selected Poems*, edited and translated by Richard Zenith, Penguin Books, 2006.

Pessoa, Fernando. *The Book of Disquiet*, edited by Pizarro Ferónimo. Translated by Margaret Full Costa, New Directions, 2017.

Pessoa, Fernando. *The Selected Prose of Fernando Pessoa*, edited and translated by Richard Zenith, Grove Press, 2002.

Pessoa, Fernando. "Quem quisesse resumir numa palavra a característica principal da arte moderna." *Arquivo Pessoa*. http://arquivopessoa.net/textos/1415. Accessed 25 Sept. 2020.

Pizarro, Jerónimo. "How to Construct a Master: Pessoa and Caeiro." *Portuguese Studies*, vol. 33, no. 1, 2017, pp. 56-69. https://www.jstor.org/stable/10.5699/ portstudies.33.1.0056.

Plato. The Republic. Translated by Benjamin Jowett. Ulan Press, 2012.

Riding Giants. Directed by Stacy Peralta, performances by Laird Hamilton, Darrick Doerner, Dave Klama, and Jeff Clark, Sony Pictures Classics, 2004.

Rorty, Richard. Contingency, irony, and solidarity. Cambridge University Press, 1989.

Rorty, Richard. Philosophy as Poetry. University of Virginia Press, 2016.

Rose, Richard. *Energy Transmutation Between-ness and Transmission.* Rose Publications, 1985.

Rose, Richard. *The Direct-Mind Experience.* Rose Publications, 1985.

Ryan, Bartholomew. "Mythologising the Exiled Self in James Joyce and Fernando Pessoa." *Brown University.* 2013. https://www.brown.edu/ Departments/Portuguese_Brazilian_Studies/ejph/pessoaplural/Issue4/ PDF/I4A04.pdf.

Schmidgen, Henning. "Münsterberg's Photoplays: Instruments and Models in his laboratories at Freiburg and Harvard (1891-1893)." *Semantic Scholar,* 2010, https://pdfs.semanticscholar.org/885d/a72138b189cd3070e8307e85db-077ccee033c.pdf.

Shklovsky, Viktor. "Art as Technique." *Justin Childress,* Aug. 2016, http://justin-childress.co/wp-content/uploads/2016/08/shklovsky1.pdf.

Silva-Mcneill, Patricia. *Yeats and Pessoa: Parallel Poetic Styles.* Legenda, 2010.

Solomons, Leon M., and Gertrude Stein. "Normal Motor Automatism." *Psychological Review,* vol. 3, no. 5, 1896, pp. 492-512. http://wexler.free.fr/ library/files/solomons%20(1896)%20normal%20motor%20automatism.pdf.

Starlin, Jim. "Metamorphosis." *Captain Marvel The Complete Collection,* Marvel Comics Group, 2016.

Stein, Gertrude. A Stein Reader. Northwestern University Press, 1993.

Stein, Gertrude. Lectures in America. Beacon Press, 1985.

Stein, Gertrude. The Autobiography of Alice B. Toklas. Vintage Books, 1990.

Stein, Gertrude. "Cultivated motor Automatism; A Study of Character in its Relation to Attention." Psychological Review, vol. 5, no. 3, 1898, pp. 295-306. https://doi. org/10.1037/h0073997.

Stein, Gertrude. "Picasso." https://www.poetrynook.com/poem/picasso. Accessed 22 Oct. 2020.

Sutin, Lawrence. *Divine Invasions: A Life of Philip K. Dick.* Carroll & Graf Publishers, 2005.

Swaminathan, Nikhil. "Why Does the Brain Need So Much Power?" *Scientific American,* 29 Apr. 2008. https://www.scientificamerican.com/article/why-does-the-brain-need-s/.

Tolstoy, Leo. *What is Art?* Translated by Pevear, Richard and Larissa Volokhonsky, Penguin Books, 1996.

Total Recall. Directed by Paul Verhoeven, performances by Arnold Schwarzenegger, Sharon Stone, Michael Ironside, Tristar Pictures, 1990.

Tymoczko, Dmitri. "The Nitrous Oxide Philosopher." *The Atlantic,* May 1996, https://www.theatlantic.com/magazine/archive/1996/05/the-nitrous-oxide-philosopher/376581/.

Walters, Dorothy. *Kundalini Wonder: The God/Goddess in your Body.* Emergence Education, 2020.

Walters, Dorothy. *Unmasking the Rose: A Record of a Kundalini Initiation.* Hampton Roads, 2002.

Whitehead, Alfred North. *Process and Reality.* The Free Press, 1978.

Whitman, Walt. *Leaves of Grass.* Oxford University Press, 2005.

Will, Barbara. *Gertrude Stein, Modernism, and the Problem of 'Genius.'* Edinburgh University Press, 2000.

Will, Barbara. "Gertrude Stein, Automatic Writing and the Mechanics of Genius." *Forum for Modern Language Studies,* vol. 37, no. 2, Apr. 2001, pp. 169-175. https://doi.org/10.1093/fmls/37.2.169.

York, Maurice, and Rick Spaulding, editors. *Natural History of the Intellect: The Last lectures of Ralph Waldo Emerson.* Wrightwood Press, 2008.

About the Author

JEFF CARREIRA IS a meditation teacher, mystical philosopher and author who works with a growing number of people throughout the world. As a teacher, he offers retreats and courses guiding individuals in a form of meditation he refers to as *The Art of Conscious Contentment*. Through this simple and effective technique, he has led thousands of people in a journey beyond the confines of fear and self-concern into the expansive liberated awareness that is our true home.

As a philosopher, Jeff is interested in defining a new way of being in the world that will move us from our current paradigm of separation and isolation into an emerging paradigm of unity and wholeness. In his books and lectures, he explores revolutionary ideas in the domains of spirituality, consciousness, and human development. He creates courses and programs that encourage people to question their most foundational experience of reality until previously held assumptions fall away leaving space for a dramatically new understanding to emerge.

Jeff is passionate about the potential ideas have to shape how we perceive reality and how we live together. His enthusiasm for learning is infectious, and he has taught at colleges and universities throughout the world.

In a world in which university education is often thought of as a vocational certificate, seeing someone obviously relishing the acquisition and sharing of knowledge for its own sake is inspiring. — Dr. William O. Shropshire, Provost and Professor Emeritus Ogelthorpe University

Jeff is the author of numerous books including *American Awakening, Philosophy Is Not a Luxury, The Soul of a New Self, Paradigm Shifting,* and *The Art of Conscious Contentment.*

For more information visit: jeffcarreira.com

how this book relates to my own
p.2 belief: expand realm of
p.3 -this book wanted to be written possu
139 Imaginal Realm

Made in the USA
Las Vegas, NV
26 April 2021